EVERYTHING ABOUT

TAROT

Learn • Explore • Practice

EVERYTHING ABOUT TAROT

Learn • Explore • Practice

MANISHA KOUSHIK

Published by
PRABHAT PRAKASHAN PVT. LTD.
4/19 Asaf Ali Road,
New Delhi-110 002 (INDIA)
e-mail: prabhatbooks@gmail.com

ISBN 978-93-5562-063-7
EVERYTHING ABOUT TAROT
by Manisha Koushik

Edition
2026

Price
₹ 400 (Rupees Four Hundred Only)

Printed at
Sita Fine Arts, Delhi

Author's Note

If you are holding this book and have a keen interest in tarot cards—you are certainly on a path of divination. The universe wants you to understand this. The curiosity in you wants to explore the magic behind these cards. But before you begin—understand that 'you' may be a chosen one to pursue this in order to help those around you or those who come to you to look for answers troubling them.

Seventy-eight magical cards in the Rider Waite tarot deck—understanding and using them to gain insights not only puts your life on track but of all others who come under their shadow . One might find them complicated since there are so many cards to learn the meaning of, and the pictures on the cards can relate to ample messages. But then my mentor, guide and father—Dr Prem Kumar Sharma, a renowned astrologer, said that if one learns a game, one should have a passion for it. Understanding these decks also needs a strong commitment and dedication. If you are in for it—I promise to be by your side to make this learning simple, fun and of course eventful.

Cards talk to you, question you, guide you, answer you, suggest to you, modify you, and do everything for you holistically. Some fortunate people get a chance to have an interactive session with them. Luckily you may be one of them. Just stick to it and get the tempo rolling!

You cannot judge the depth of the sea without going inside it—in the same way, to know about the mysterious powers of these cards, you need to dig your hands into them. You must understand their eloquent nature and pay complete reverence to them.

Some tips for you

When you are a learner—you focus more on mastering the science than learning the rules that make the learning stronger. Thus, it is very important to pay attention to this set of rules that can bring in more accuracy and of course great results for your hard work. Let us understand them:

The deck you purchase should only be used by you. This means keeping them safe and away from anyone else's reach so that others do not touch or use them.

To bar the negativity of the cards from affecting you, always keep them covered in a cloth and place them in a storage box. I usually keep the cards in a red velvet pouch, then wrap that pouch in a small red velvet cloth on which the cards can be laid. While I am travelling, I keep this entire pack safe in a wooden box.

While learning them, reading them, or looking at them—one must observe silence to focus completely on them.

As a learner, you need to spend a couple of hours to acquaint yourself with the energies of the cards as well as while learning the book. Avoid distractions of any sort.

Just like a student, you should have all your accessories with you like pen, pencil and paper, accompanied by cards. A neat and clean diary can be maintained for the observations or instant intuitions that you make by looking at the cards while learning or reading for a person.

❑

Acknowledgements

Writing this book has been an incredible journey, and I feel overwhelmed with gratitude for the unwavering support and love I have received from my family, friends, and well-wishers. Their encouragement and participation in this journey have made it memorable and rewarding.

I am deeply grateful to Maa Durga for her boundless blessings and for guiding me through this journey with her unwavering grace and love. Her divine presence has been a source of strength, helping me overcome all the challenges that came my way.

I would also like to express my heartfelt thanks to my father, mentor, and guide Dr Prem Kumar Sharma, for his continuous support, guidance, and inspiration. His trust in me has given me the confidence to bring accuracy and consistency in my work with resilience and determination.

My better half, Vinay, has been my constant cheerleader, pushing me to do better and achieve more. His unwavering support, love, patience and understanding have been the cornerstones of my success, and I am incredibly grateful to have him in my life.

Last but not least, special thanks go out to my son, Nishchay, whose cooperation and untiring faith in me have been the driving force behind this endeavour. His encouragement and support have given me the strength to pursue my dreams confidently.

In conclusion, I owe my success to the love, support and guidance of all those who have played a role in my journey. Thank you for being there for me and participating in this incredible journey.

❑

Contents

Introduction

It can be a little overwhelming to sort through the wealth of material available if you are interested in reading the tarot cards. This study will help you create a fundamental framework for future academic endeavours. Tarot history, deck selection and maintenance, card meanings, and some easy spreads to attempt are some of the subjects covered in this book.

This study guide is intended to provide you with many of the fundamental working concepts you will need to continue studying in earnest later on, even though there is no replacement for actual hands-on experience. Consider this as the base upon which you can later construct.

Step 1: Getting started in Tarot

Let us begin! The first rule is to read the book word by word and page by page. If you skip any words or pages, you tend to break the algorithm of energies that you would be building within you to relate with the cards.

Avoid being in a rush to learn. You will eventually learn if you are committed and connect with your tarot cards daily.

Do not jump to conclusions before you have completely gone through a reading multiple times. It may often happen that you may get different messages in a set of readings. That is the time when you must trust your inner self to decode and intuit what your actual findings are. Meditation and a strong inner sense are also important when you do readings. It is alright, in case you feel you aren't too strong right now with your inner self—meditating daily with the cards and on the cards would help you bring that strength.

A brief history of Tarot

Although tarot cards have been used for many years now, their origin is still unknown. The word 'Tarot' is supposed to have derived from the Indo-European name of Primal Goddess Tara (Mother Earth) equivalent to Terra Mater (Latin), Terah (Hebrew), and Turan (Etruscan). Also, Tar-Ro means the 'royal road' in Egyptian.

Which cards to choose?

A few tasks are confusing for a novice tarot reader—like selecting their first tarot deck. There are numerous tarot cards to choose from. It might even feel a bit overpowering. I always suggest referring to the Rider Waite deck, to begin with, since it is one of the most authentic and oldest versions of tarot cards.

Keep your cards safe

Congratulations! You have successfully discovered the tarot deck that resonates with you. What should you do with them now that you have brought them home? Learn how to 'charge' your cards to shield them from harm and negative energy. Sit with them daily—hold them in your hands—look at them carefully and try to connect with them. After this exercise, shuffle them and wrapping them in a cloth, keep them in a box.

Step 2: Get ready to read your cards

So, precisely how does one conduct a tarot reading? To begin with, you should get yourself and your cards ready before you begin. Let's go over some of the information you will need to understand the cards themselves.

Interpreting the cards

The true reading starts now that you have put down your tarot cards. If someone approaches you in the capacity of a querent, it is because they want to know what is happening while also seeking out an engaging story. Anyone can read in a book that the Ten of Cups represents contentment and pleasure, after all. How it specifically relates to them is all they are interested in knowing.

Step 3: Learn the meanings!

Learn the representations of the cards, but do not simply cram or mug them. Read them multiple times. Look at the cards—does it connect with you in some new way? Maybe a new message? A new keyword? Or a new meaning that was never interpreted before? If yes, make a note of it. Come back to it later. Look at the card again (maybe after a couple of days). Are you still in sync with the first interpretation you made? Take a strong note of it and try using it in your reading to explore what more it brings along!

Step 4: Which spread to follow?

You will be introduced to multiple spreads in the last few chapters. These are the popular spreads used worldwide. It is good to learn, understand and know about them. You may even use all of them for your readings.

Step 5: Major and Minor Arcana

These are the anchors of tarot card reading and understanding them is very important. Broadly they can be understood like this—Major Arcana talks about major stages or the important external influences in life, while Minor Arcana talks about minor decisions or small chores or everyday actions.

Step 6: Court cards

Court cards are the touchstones that can help one decide which way to proceed. Though confusing, they have many faithful messages in them. You should concoct a unique method of analysing them to impress your clients. And after their positive feedback, you can try all the aspects yourself.

❑

CHAPTER 1

Basics of Tarot

Let us begin with learning about the cards. Many tarot decks are available in the market and it is tough to choose one. The best way to start with is the oldest and the most traditional tarot deck, the Rider Waite tarot deck. It has good illustrations and is widely used. Apart from this, decks are of different assortments, depending on their quantity, names and patterns.

Rider Waite tarot cards are a pack of a total of 78 cards which in general are divided into two categories. Remember, learning is directly proportional to your hard work; the more you will research, the more you will discover.

Every Rider Waite deck has two legs:

1. The Major Arcana has 22 cards.
2. The Minor Arcana has 56 cards.

You must be pondering over your first technical term "Arcana". Arcana means "Confidential" and each card can be called as "Arcanum". It was derived from a latin word arcanus, meaning "secret" and was broadly used in reference to the mysteries of the physical and spiritual worlds.

Introduction of the first leg, i.e., Major Arcana

Each card is a numbered card and the numbers on the Major Arcana cards start from 0 to 21 (Total 22 Cards). Each card, in itself, is a short tale or a short text which tells about your most substantial situations in life, and your reaction at that time, pragmatically, emotionally and spiritually, in a reading. On the contrary, the second leg, i.e., the Minor Arcana, presents your day-to-day activities in a reading.

Different decks have their own arrangement of cards that people follow. So, a card with some number in one deck might have another number in another. To avoid this confusion, let's stick to only the Rider Waite deck and consider the numbers for reference. Although in some decks, the Justice card comes ahead of the Strength card and hence has a different number from the list below:

The table shows cards of Major Arcana ascribing their respective element, planet, or zodiac sign.

0 – The Fool	Uranus, Air
1 – The Magician	Mercury, Air
2 – The High Priestess	Moon, Water
3 – The Empress	Venus, Earth
4 – The Emperor	Aries, Fire
5 – The Hierophant	Taurus, Earth
6 – The Lovers	Gemini, Air

7 – The Chariot	Cancer, Water
8 – Strength	Leo, Fire
9 – The Hermit	Virgo, Earth
10 – Wheel of Fortune	Jupiter, Fire
11 – Justice	Libra, Air
12 – The Hanged Man	Water, Neptune
13 – Death	Scorpio, Water
14 – Temperance	Sagittarius, Fire
15 – The Devil	Capricorn, Earth
16 – The Tower	Mars, Fire
17 – The Star	Aquarius, Air
18 – The Moon	Pisces, Water
19 – The Sun	Sun, Fire
20 – Judgement	Pluto, Fire
21 – The World	Saturn, Earth

Since the first card that we see in the Major Arcana is The Fool, 'Fool's Journey' is the name given to the cards of this set of the deck. The quest is to transform the initial state of 'sentience (depicted by card numbered 0)' to the final state of 'satisfaction (shown by card numbered 21)'.

The cards clearly display the timbers with which we are born to the qualities we imbibe in our life with the passage of time. In short, it is the complete biography of the emotions that we show at different points in time, the state of health that we possess, our connection with those around us, and most importantly channelising the energies from the universe.

Further, Major Arcana is bifurcated into two parts. The centre state is called 'Wheel of Fortune'. This stage describes the transition from awakening in the past to awakening in the future. It also depicts your upcoming flourishing time.

Second leg, i.e., the Minor Arcana

This leg is divided into four parts: namely Wands, Cups, Swords and Pentacles. It is much like playing cards.

Some decks may call them by different names too. Variations in the name of the parts might be like this:

Wands are also known as Rods or Batons.

Pentacles are also known as Coins or Discs.

Since we are sticking with the Rider Waite deck, let's understand them as—Wands, Cups, Swords and Pentacles. Each part has 10 cards on which numerals are displayed from 1 to 10 and 4 court cards namely: Page, Knight, Queen and King.

Queen – an adult woman of any age

King – a man aged 35 or over

Knight – a man aged under 35

Page – a male or female child or adolescent

Elements and signs related to each part according to astrology are:

Wands – Fire – Aries, Leo, Sagittarius

Cups – Water – Cancer, Scorpio, Pisces

Swords – Air – Gemini, Libra, Aquarius

Pentacles- Earth- Taurus, Virgo, Capricorn

- ✦ **Wands:** show the graph of your professional life, commitment and dedication to your task, and artistic nature.
- ✦ **Cups:** are related to your emotions and relationships and show how you are placed emotionally—strong or weak?

- ✦ **Swords:** display your intelligence and generic view of everything.
- ✦ **Pentacles:** are associated with your monetary status and luxuries you want in your life.

The learning doesn't stop here. There's more to it. We have just begun understanding what we are going to talk in detail about.

Points to ponder

Now you have some hands-on knowledge about the cards. Start analysing them and spend some time with your notes. I understand how curious you would be to start exploring the cards for prediction but my suggestion is—Avoid performing any readings till you are through with the entire book.

But you can definitely do this:

1. Try connecting with the energies of these cards by shuffling them multiple times in a day.
2. Try relating with your own self—Which court card is your astrological card?

❑

CHAPTER 2

Detailed Introduction of Major Arcana

The Major Arcana: Session 1

Does the curiosity grow further? Did you have a look at the Major Arcana cards carefully? If you have any observations on seeing the cards, or you feel this card is trying to give a message, make a separate note of it. Consider this for future reference. You will be soon in a position to describe each and every card in your unique way rather than depending on my observations or any other literature.

The best way to learn about the cards is to read through the literature and then couple it with your own experiences. I have tried to gather both for you in this book. It may sound theoretical in nature, but it is largely based on my practical experience with the cards. This will provide you with a strong base, but you must prove the idiom 'Experience and knowledge result in better judgement' for yourself. Try to develop the confidence to interpret things at your level.

Now that we have begun learning about the Major Arcana Cards, we will divide them into two parts:

3. The journey from The Fool (0) to Wheel of Fortune (10)
4. The journey from Justice (11) to The World (21)

What I want you to focus on in this chapter is the chart we mentioned above. Read it as many times as possible to memorise the names, their astrological signs and elements. Trust me, once these things are clear in your mind, you will be able to perform great readings.

We will cover the astrological associations and relevance of the cards in the upcoming chapters. But for now, let's understand the reason for memorising them. It can be used as a guide for timing.

The relationship between the astrological dates and their respective Major Arcana cards can be learnt from the table shown below.

The time period from 21st March to 19th April will be related to The Emperor in the spread if it comes ahead of all. For more understanding, look at the table:

Number	Card Title	Astrological Sign	Dates
4	The Emperor	Aries	21 March - 19 April
5	The Hierophant	Taurus	20 April - 20 May
6	The Lovers	Gemini	21 May - 21 June
7	The Chariot	Cancer	22 June - 22 July

8	Strength	Leo	23 July - 22 August
9	The Hermit	Virgo	23 August - 22 September
11	Justice	Libra	23 September - 23 October
13	Death	Scorpio	24 October - 21 November
14	Temperance	Sagittarius	22 November - 21 December
15	The Devil	Capricorn	22 December - 19 January
17	The Star	Aquarius	20 January - 18 February
18	The Moon	Pisces	19 February - 20 March

Try some exercises based on previous learning:

- What does Major Arcana represent?
- How many cards are there in it?
- What is their impact on our life or how do they influence us?
- What is 'Wheel of Fortune' and what does it imply?

You should be very clear with these topics before proceeding, else the things we learn further will only confuse you.

Major Arcana as said is related to the peak time of your life, so cautiously read, predict and experience it. You will learn more in the upcoming chapters on spreads.

Journey from The Fool (0) to Wheel of Fortune (10)

Moving further, the next step is to unpack the cards numbered (0) to (10) from the deck. It is time to discover the hidden truth behind these cards. Be careful while placing the rest of the cards back in the box. I always keep my cards covered in a red velvet cloth and lay the cards on the same cloth for a reading; its energies are just wonderful.

Make sure the pile of cards is in systematic tandem and that you only focus on one card at a time.

Every card has a vibe associated with it for you to learn from and learn about. Be it a card from the Major Arcana or Minor Arcana—it will have one significant energy to relate with. These energies will provide more meaning to the cards as you start seeing them in your readings often.

The easiest way to learn them is to read the name on the card with its corresponding word and memorise it. Try to make assumptions on your own and write down what comes to your mind concerning both the effects, i.e., good and bad. The figure in the card, the word, the vibes, be it good or bad, will definitely bewitch you. Try to hear what they are saying to you.

Different people have different ways of working. Some grasp things quickly, and some take time. So, learn at your own pace; don't be in a hurry. Do not get stressed or worried if you take more than a week to cover this exercise, as mere reading will not serve the purpose.

When you have finished studying the notes, then refer to the keywords to know about the detailed importance of each card.

Card 0: The Fool

Card 1: The Magician

Card 2: The High Priestess

Card 3: The Empress

Card 4: The Emperor

Card 5: The Hierophant

Card 6: The Lovers

Card 7: The Chariot

Card 8: Strength

Card 9: The Hermit

Card 10: Wheel of Fortune

The Major Arcana: Session 2

Keep up the spirit and get going…

You need to form a rigid stance to act on the standards of these cards. If the data provided here gives you clarity about the nature of the cards, then congratulations! You are on the right track. If you sense the energy, stamina and immunity of these cards, then consider yourself lucky that the cards are supporting your intention to learn and interact with them.

If you find the information a bit tricky to mug up and feel some difficulty in adopting the modes and practices of these cards, then stay calm. This domain is easy to learn but demands time from your side. To work according to your own capability is the key to success. Information will be available round the clock and is one click away from you.

You need to develop a strong bond with the cards for a smooth relationship with them. Merely cramming and spouting the information will not serve the purpose.

You have to frame your mind and bow down to the manipulation of each and every card of your deck. While learning, you will feel that a relationship is also established between you and your soul that is often a spiritual connection between your inner self and higher self.

To keep things in tandem, I have portrayed the information here in the same way as in session 1. There needs to be a synchronised flow of facts.

You are supposed to follow the ethics of the school where after a reading, you will be given an exercise. I am sure the whole session will result in a flashback to your childhood days.

To cultivate all the blessings of the cards, you need to feel them with full force. Keep your senses activated all the time.

Be alert and thoroughly observe what's going on around you during the reading of the cards.

Description of the cards from Card 11 (Justice) to Card 21 (The World):

This set of cards depicts that your life seems stressful, your task list is growing, and work is alarming or unsatisfactory. You must fight against all odds to get the taste of success or to rebuild your morale.

'Handle with care' is what describes this pile of cards. Your academic skills, technical knowledge, artistic nature and inner zeal—all are required to read these cards. You must correctly interpret the significance of their meanings, else you will lose your way.

For a formal introduction, take these cards (cards numbered 11 to 21) out of the deck and place the rest of the cards gently covered inside the box.

Every card can be a boon or bane for you. To discover it, go through the semantics behind the figure shown on the card. Read what is good or bad for you.

Avoid a fast and furious attitude. Learn according to your will and power. If you force yourself, then it might turn out to be a useless activity. Spend a considerable amount of time on them. Accumulate all your energy to continue with the cards.

Activate your intuition and focus on the cards. Make a note of each keyword that you come across.

11 - Justice

12 – The Hanged Man

13 – Death

14 – Temperance

15 – The Devil

16 – The Tower

17 – The Star

18 – The Moon

19 – The Sun

20 – Judgement

21 – The World

Card 0: The Fool

Element: Air

Planet: Uranus/Rahu

Upright: New prospects, positive energy, dynamic, audacious, passionate, imaginative, jovial, discoverer

Reversed: Careless, impatient, lack of sophistication, lack of thoughts, childish behaviour, anarchy

Card description: The Fool is depicted as a young man who exudes confidence and fearlessly ventures into the world. He is brimming with enthusiasm and is taking his first steps on his journey with a boundless supply of energy and happiness. Despite the potential hazards lurking ahead, he appears oblivious to them and carries only a small sack on his shoulder. One such peril is looming close. He is dangerously close to falling off the cliff in front of him with just one more step. Nevertheless, he seems unfazed, and it's unclear whether he is simply ignorant or intentionally reckless. A dog follows closely behind him, reminding him to be careful and not take unnecessary risks lest he misses out on the thrilling opportunities he seeks.

Number association: This card is numbered 0. It can indicate infinite possibilities. Some people put it before the deck, and others consider it the last card. Remember, 0 does not have any value of its own. But it will add value to any number when it sits beside it. Similarly, when this card is next to any Major Arcana card, it will add value/strength to that card. Though if occurring with a Minor Arcana card, it holds its own importance and stands out in the set of cards.

Personal growth: You are about to embark on an adventure that could take a long time. Allow your intuition and fate to lead you. Experience is an excellent teacher, and you may be in for some pleasant surprises along the way. Maintain an open mind and faith that everything will turn out fine. Do not be concerned; instead, rejoice!

About a person: The Fool represents someone who is a child at heart. They may be fun-loving, trusting and naive. They go with the flow, blissfully oblivious of the risks or obstacles that lie ahead on life's road. If present as a negative card or as the first card in a reading, the person could be unreliable and may not take life seriously.

Money: When dealing with money, you might be immature or naive. If you are thinking about investing, look into it thoroughly, pay attention to the small print, and ensure you have all the information you need. The Fool can also symbolise the start of a financial or business venture.

Love: Unexpected circumstances may have led to a 'destined' connection; approach it with innocence, faith, and an open heart. As you embark on a new romance or a new phase of a long-term relationship, be spontaneous and enthusiastic.

Career: The Fool denotes the beginning of a new employment, career path, or business endeavour. Approach the issue with an open mind and a positive attitude, eager to take advantage of chances as they arise.

Important: The card appearing before a Fool card in a reading would have more value. It will suggest how eventful the Fool is going to be. It may also represent whether you are on the right or wrong track.

Card 1: The Magician

Element: Air

Planet: Mercury

Upright: Strength, purity, pride, self-satisfied, desirous, capable, energetic

Reversed: Profoundness in language, bilk, wily, deceitful, weak

Card description: The Magician is particularly rich in symbolism. The man appears to be saying 'as above, so below' with one hand raised to the heavens and the other pointing to the ground. Earth is a reflection of heaven; the outer world is a reflection of the inner world; the microcosm is a reflection of the macrocosm; and God is reflected on the earth. In this context, the Magician may also stand for the capacity to mediate between the spiritual realm and our own modern reality.

The Magician also has the symbols of the tarot suits—a cup, pentacle, sword and wand arranged on his table. This is a metaphor for the connection of earth, water, air and fire by this magician. Infinity represents the boundless potential of the human will to create.

Number association: This card is numbered 1, which means that it has the power to be supreme over anything else. Whatever the situation, you will get through it and surprise everyone with the best of your abilities.

Personal growth: Instead of allowing someone else to influence you, take charge of your life and surroundings. Align yourself with Divine Will, and channel the energy of the universe to manifest the results you want.

About a person: The Magician denotes someone who is secretive, private, and untrustworthy at times. This individual prefers to work in the background, manipulating events to acquire power and influence. If surrounded by all negative cards, they could be a con artist who preys on individuals and situations. On a positive note, this card could imply someone with highly developed psychic or magical abilities.

Money: You have the ability to make money by effectively utilising your skills. Increase your riches by utilising the global flow. This card could also indicate that you or someone else is working behind the scenes or exploiting resources that aren't readily available.

Love: In a relationship, there could be concerns about control, manipulation, or power. Maybe you're in a power struggle, and one or both are playing games. Seek a win-win arrangement rather than stubbornly attempting to grab an advantage.

Career: Someone could be working behind your back to obtain power and control or manipulating a circumstance to achieve their goals. There may be power battles. Keep a close eye on your surroundings and avoid getting involved in anything risky. Keep your secrets hidden.

Card 2: The High Priestess

Element: Water

Planet: Moon

Upright: Spontaneous, non-rational, comprehending, charismatic, sharp mind, closed book

Reversed: Dissonance, keep things hidden, static, highly possessive

Card description: The High Priestess is an archetype that you have likely encountered before in the figures of Persephone, Artemis, Isis, and countless others. She is seated between the two pillars of Solomon's Temple, Jachin and Boaz, on a cube-shaped stone. Boaz (meaning 'strength)' on the left is black , and Jachin on the right (meaning 'he will establish') is white. The pillars signify male and female, light and dark, positive and negative, all dual aspects of nature.

The High Priestess stands at the threshold between the two, implying that it is her role to mediate between the two layers of reality. She's the middle ground, the link between the other two. From her perspective, there is something to be gained from studying both fields. A believer in the supernatural, as suggested by her crown of Isis, is another possible interpretation. The solar cross on her chest symbolises her closeness to the changing of the seasons and the planet itself. The priestess's ambition is symbolised by the pomegranates on her veil, and her emotional stability is represented by the crescent moon at her feet, which is also seen in many depictions of the Virgin Mary.

Number association: Number 2 is ruled by the Moon in numerology. Moon represents the mother, feelings, intuition, water, mood and our sensitive side. This number is known to bring about team spirit, work in collaboration and most importantly, be a peacemaker in situations of discord.

Personal growth: Pay attention to your intuition and look inward. Develop your inherent talents as well as your spiritual side.

About a person: The High Priestess is a spiritual or esoteric figure with intuitive abilities. This individual may be lonely or reclusive, maybe because the stress of a busy, public life is too much for them to handle.

Money: In a financial problem, the High Priestess advises you to trust your gut. This card may also indicate that you are too 'other worldly' and could benefit from becoming more practical with your money and belongings.

Love: Your intuition about a relationship or a companion is often correct. Rather than trying to examine a person or love situation too closely, listen to your heart and let your feelings guide you.

Career: Listen to your inner voice and follow its advice when making decisions at work. Trust your instincts, and practical answers and rational analysis. The presence of the High Priestess may also be interpreted as a warning to investigate the inner workings of a situation rather than taking things at face value.

Card 3: The Empress

Element: Earth

Planet: Venus

Season: Spring

Upright: Productive, affectionate, humorous, flourishing, creative, motherhood

Reversed: Tussles on the home front, losing confidence, sentimental, over-caring, dearth of money, sterility, physical intimacy without any commitment

Card description: The Empress card depicts a woman, wearing a crown, sitting on a throne. Given the thriving environment, this woman probably represents Earth, the Mother archetype, a goddess of fertility. Venus is the planet of love, harmony, fertility and luxury, and her realm enjoys all four thanks to her beneficence. It is a sign of the woman's divine and mystical connection that she wears a crown adorned with stars on her blonde head. She is clad in a robe emblazoned with pomegranates, a symbol of fertility, and is perched on cushions emblazoned with the symbol of Venus. A beautiful green forest with a river running through it surrounds her. When the Empress visits a town, everyone she comes in contact with receives a reading full of good fortune and prosperity.

Number association: This card is ruled by Venus but its number vibrations are that of Jupiter. Number 3 represents the planet Jupiter in numerology. Jupiter is said to be Dev Guru (Mentor of Gods), and Venus is said to be Daitya Guru (Mentor of Demons). Although it gives the native all luxuries of life and blesses them with the happiness that one desires, it also keeps them always in a state of confusion. The decision-making power may be slow, and one may not be able to come to a closure or conclusion soon.

Personal growth: Whether you are a man or a woman, the Empress signifies feminine power and encourages you to explore your feminine side. Meditate on this card to boost creativity, inspiration, and emotional equilibrium.

About a person: The Empress is a mature figure who understands her worth, a self-assured and hard-working woman. This person is frequently motivated and inventive. She enthusiastically supports others' endeavours and is a source of inspiration for those she meets.

Money: The Empress is a symbol of sound financial and material management. A collaboration or collaborative project may be beneficial to you. You will have good luck and financial stability. This card may also indicate that you need to increase your self-worth or place a greater emphasis on your abilities.

Love: The Empress denotes a mature, rational outlook. You are serious about love and want to be in a relationship built on mutual respect, trust, deep affection, giving and taking. You have genuine feelings and are willing to commit to a partner. The Empress can suggest a strong, devoted and accomplished mate who matches a man's romantic ideal in a reading.

Career: Teamwork is essential at this time, and creative relationships may be beneficial to you. Use your abilities to benefit yourself and others in a sensible and responsible manner. Execute a work or project to the best of your ability and ingenuity.

Card 4: The Emperor

Astrological sign: Aries

Element: Fire

Upright: Glorious, dominating, helpful, loyal, committed, strong, passionate, disciplined

Reversed: Fickle, dictator, prone to luxuries, careless, not responsible, without aim

Card description: The Emperor tarot card depicts a stoic ruler sitting atop a throne adorned with the horns of four rams, each horn corresponding to one of the four elements associated with the Aries zodiac sign. He holds the sceptre in the right hand, a symbol of his rule and authority, while the orb in the left hand represents the realm he maintains order over. The Emperor's long beard is a symbol of his wisdom and experience. He has learnt much about what it takes to rule, establish power, authority, and complete order for the good of his people.

The stark mountains in the background symbolise his grit, drive and potential as a leader. The Empress, whose sweeping fields overflow with nurturing kindness, is the polar opposite. However, the Emperor rules with an iron will and unyielding strength.

Number association: Number 4 is all about organising things and bringing order and discipline to life. They cannot withstand disrespecting commitments. If representing a situation, you may not be even halfway through right now, and many twists and turns may yet come; although the victory will be yours eventually.

Personal growth: Make a conscious effort to be more responsible and realistic. Meditate on this card to improve self-esteem, confidence, and physical/material grounding.

About a person: The Emperor is usually a mature person, possibly a father figure, who holds a position of power. In general, the card denotes a practical person who is a good manager, businessman or works in the financial sector. He's a strong, stable person who can be counted on for sound advice, support, and advancement.

Money: To ensure your situation is solid and secure, manage your finances carefully. As you vigorously pursue your goals, be efficient and practical. In a business, legal matter, estate, or other ventures with a known person, you may be entrusted with money and/or material assets. You will get the opportunity to succeed in financial matters.

Love: The Emperor represents a mature and sensible approach to relationships. It can sometimes reveal a connection primarily motivated by money or practical factors. This card can imply a steady, financially secure, and mature male partner in a woman's reading, but one who may be emotionally unresponsive.

Career: Organisation, accountability and order should all be prioritised. Make your workplace more stable and structured. It's possible that you'll need a business plan or a well-functioning system. It's possible that you'll have to take on additional responsibilities or lead others. This card could represent a job in business, law, finance or management.

Card 5: The Hierophant

Planet: Earth

Astrological sign: Taurus

Upright: Highly intellectual, an example for others, respectful, trustworthy, religious, highly recognised

Reversed: Crook, chaos in mind, distract others, complex in nature to understand, lack of knowledge

Card description: The card features a religious figure seated between two pillars of a sacred temple. He is dressed in three robes to represent the three realms (the subconscious, conscious and super-conscious). He raises his right hand in a gesture of benediction and blessing. He also has a triple cross, a symbol of the papacy, in his other hand. The horizontal arms of the cross are often taken to symbolise the Trinity (the Father, the Son, and the Holy Spirit). Two acolytes sit at his feet, a symbol of the transmission of religious teachings within a given organisation. As a result of its adherents, the card has come to symbolise gaining insight and education.

In some decks, this card is also known as the Pope or High Priest. In this role, he is the masculine counterpart to the High Priestess. Taurus is the star sign associated with this card.

Number association: Number 5 represents Mercury in numerology. Mercury is known to be the fastest-moving planet that orbits around the sun. It is known to be the prince in the astrology kingdom and thus gathers all the love and attention from those around it. They are quick decision-makers and someone who doesn't take problems too seriously. They have a short attention span but have immense curiosity to learn about things. Change is another attribute of this number.

Personal growth: You're having a hard time learning a lesson. Wisdom comes from experience, and life's great truths are frequently revealed through struggle and pain. Learn the purpose of a challenge by meditating on it.

About a person: The Hierophant is a well-known authority or leader, usually a teacher or someone who works in the spiritual realm. This individual may be able to interpret laws, customs, religion or cultural beliefs. They are frequently someone from whom you can seek advice.

Money: You can make money using your expertise, but you'll have to follow certain rules and restrictions. Maybe you should look into your attitude towards money—do you believe that having money isn't spiritual? The Hierophant could also indicate that you should focus on spiritual truths rather than material concerns.

Love: The Hierophant represents a relationship's most spiritual aspects. You and your spouse may have a common purpose or be committed to a greater good. Your connection gets the best out of both of you. This card represents personal love as a spiritual quest or route to divine love. It could also signify a secure relationship with clearly defined boundaries, such as marriage or a steady partnership.

Career: You may need to follow the rules or work inside a pre-existing framework to make progress. Working on a subject involving knowledge, religion, or long-standing traditions can be associated with the Hierophant. It can also suggest that you integrate your spiritual path with work.

Card 6: The Lovers

Astrological sign: Gemini

Element: Air

Upright: Excitement, eagerness, relations, emotions, physical pleasure, firm promises, affairs

Reversed: Disunion, mental harassment, loss of money and time, feelings of loneliness, maligned image, loss of character

Card description: The card shows an angel blessing the man and woman standing beneath. The couple stand in a beautiful garden that appears to be paradise. The woman stands with her back to a fruit tree with a snake on its trunk, alluding to the myth about humanity's descent into the realm of the senses. Raphael, the angel of air, is depicted here, and the element of air is also associated with the zodiac sign Gemini, which rules this card. Connections built on open lines of communication are the bedrock of any flourishing social system, and this is why air is so closely linked to the workings of the mind. It's as if the angel's blessing lends this card a sense of equilibrium and harmony, representing a cosmically significant union of seemingly opposing forces.

Number association: Number 6 represents the planet Venus, known for love and attraction. Thus this card may indicate a period of self-love, love between two people, and attraction towards the opposite sex. Number 6 may also represent luxuries and material things that bring you happiness.

Personal growth: This card can indicate a time period when your inner and outer natures are in sync. To connect your masculine and feminine aspects, meditate on The Lovers.

About a person: This indicates affection and harmony among the couple. It could also refer to someone who has qualities you don't have and can help you out. This card can also represent a marriage counsellor, mediator, or agent who works to reconcile disagreements and bring people together.

Money: Joining forces with a business partner could be advantageous. You may benefit from the resources of a spouse or partner. This card may also indicate that you will acquire funding for a project or business venture. The Lovers bring luck, especially when working together.

Love: This card depicts a mutually beneficial connection. You and your lover have a happy, harmonious relationship that brings out the best in you. When it comes to love, The Lovers may encourage you to decide.

Career: Partnerships, joint enterprises and teamwork may be beneficial. Bring pragmatism and creativity together. This card shows that cooperation and collaboration may be better than selfishness or competitiveness.

Card 7: The Chariot

Astrological sign: Cancer

Element: Water

Upright: Control, success, confidence, a one-man army, bold, cheerful news

Reversed: Jealous, deceiving, dominating, mean, attitude, mental trauma, irritation

Card description: The Chariot card shows a human figure atop a chariot pulled by two sphinxes, one black and one white. The card takes on a heavenly tone, with the man sitting under a blue canopy dotted with white stars. The crescent moon, symbolising the higher power that directs his life, rests on his shoulder. A crown rests on his head, an emblem of his enlightenment and the purity of his intent. A square is emblazoned across his tunic, representing the element of earth and the material world that serves as a foundation for him and his decisions.

The sphinxes are depicted in black and white to represent competing forces that the charioteer must master. They appear to be calm but frequently fight because they want to go in different directions. These sphinxes are under his charge to arrive at a specific location, as designated by the cosmic forces he embodies.

The Cancer zodiac sign is associated with the Chariot.

Number association: Number 7 represents Neptune in numerology and Ketu as per Vedic numerology. It calls for research and a curiosity to learn about everything this person comes in touch with. You may feel stuck with a person, thought, or a situation that may be unresolved till you do not let it go.

Personal growth: Patience and detachment are two qualities that the Chariot advises. Don't be concerned about how things will turn out; trust that you will arrive on time. It is like a period of pregnancy; each one is different and adds to various experiences; learn all you can. Make the best use of your strength.

About a Person: The Chariot could indicate someone in charge or in a position of authority. This individual may currently have power over your life.

Money: Things cannot be rushed. A financial position may take time to improve, or an investment may take time to grow. In the meantime, focus on related issues and make good use of your efforts. This card may also suggest that you take control of the situation and exert influence over the forces at work.

Love: This isn't the ideal moment for a relationship. The right person hasn't yet entered your life. Please don't give up. Perhaps you should devote time to self-improvement or other activities before getting into a relationship. This card may also suggest that you concentrate on your chosen path.

Career: You must wait for the appropriate time to make a move. Do not attempt to hasten the development of things. Take advantage of this opportunity to gain knowledge, skills, or experience. Concentrate all of your energy on your aim. You build power by controlling your over-enthusiasm and impatience. While you wait, keep an eye on what's going on and listen closely; you'll be able to put what you learn here to good use later.

Card 8: Strength

Astrological sign: Leo

Element: Fire

Upright: Has power, self-command, ecstasy, conquer, brave, audacious, kind towards needy

Reversed: Lacks courage, failure, dreadful, lazy, miss chances to grow

Card description: The Strength card portrays a woman stroking a powerful lion's jaws. Despite the lion's formidable strength and dangerous nature, the woman appears to be in complete control. The grace and finesse with which she handles the lion is truly captivating. Her calm and collected demeanour suggests that she is a responsible and rule-abiding individual, even when faced with adversity.

Moreover, her act of holding the lion's jaws is indicative of her bravery. She demonstrates love and care by keeping the lion under control without resorting to excessive force. The blue sky over the mountains in the background signifies stability and the sense of peace that comes with it.

The lion is a representation of essential human traits such as courage, passion and desire, all of which are crucial for survival. However, if left unchecked, these emotions can lead to our downfall. Therefore, this card serves as a reminder that we must always strive to control our impulses and channel them in a positive direction.

Number association: Number 8 can become rigid and hard-hearted. It is a number often linked with pain and struggle. Thus whenever this card appears, the first suggestion it gives is to be a little flexible in your approach and have patience.

Personal growth: You could be held back by negativity and/or old behaviours. It is time to stand on your own two feet and break free from the constraints you've placed on yourself. Meditate on this card to boost your self-assurance, determination, and courage.

About a person: In the face of hardship, Strength refers to someone who has inner strength, self-confidence, perseverance and fearlessness. This individual does not need to employ force to convey a point; instead, they lead by example and inspires people's trust.

Money: You should overcome the barriers and worries preventing you from succeeding. Stop relying on others and begin to support yourself. Use the inner resources you have to succeed financially.

Love: Even when things appear challenging, stay strong and persevere. Someone you care about might push you to try something new. It's possible that you'll have to drop your defences, self-limiting attitudes, and old behaviours. To get happiness and peace, you must overcome your ego, doubts and worries.

Career: You may need to tackle deep-seated fears or beliefs holding you back in order to achieve. When it comes to these problems, be bold. You can achieve a lot if you overcome your flaws. You may need to summon your inner power to deal with a tricky work-related issue. Don't give up!

Card 9: The Hermit

Astrological sign: Virgo

Element: Earth

Upright: Cool-minded, self-guided and motivated, has careful thoughts, helps others to grow

Reversed: Has mind with a negative attitude and frustration, rude, harsh, hot-headed, stubborn, fishy

Card description: The Hermit card depicts an aged gentleman who stands at the peak of a mountain, holding a lantern in one hand and a staff in the other. The mountain, standing tall and majestic, serves as a representation of success, growth and accomplishment. As the name suggests, The Hermit card is symbolic of the individual's mastery of spiritual wisdom, which he is eager to impart to others. The Hermit is highly focused on his goal and is well aware of the path he must take to achieve it.

The lantern held by The Hermit contains a six-pointed star, which is known as the Seal of Solomon. This symbol is indicative of great knowledge and enlightenment. The staff in The Hermit's hands represents his power and authority, highlighting his ability to lead and guide others towards their own personal growth and development.

Number association: Number 9 represents the planet Mars. Mars is known as a warrior—full of energy, committed to his work, and sincere with his duties. He only works at his master's command—the rest of the decisions are his own. He takes complete accountability for what he thinks and what he does.

Personal growth: The Hermit is a loner, a solitary individual who follows his or her own set of rules. This individual is self-sufficient and does not seek approval from others. Through personal experience and soul-searching, the Hermit's philosophy of life has been perfected.

About a person: Withdraw from the outside world's activity and focus on yourself. You must discover your own truth, and forced seclusion, meditation, and simplifying your life, are frequently the only ways to do it. Make some time for yourself, even if you can't drop all of your commitments.

Money: Become more self-sufficient by learning to live alone. This card may indicate a period of seclusion from the materialistic world so that you can focus on your inner life or spiritual path. Money may not appear to be a significant factor in your life right now. The Hermit might also advise you to let go of a money problem.

Love: Being alone for some time may aid in the development of your ideas, talents or self-confidence. You may choose solitary living over socialising or being with a companion. Even if you're in a relationship, your main attention right now is on you and your own journey.

Career: In order to grow and understand what is truly important to you, you must be self-sufficient. This card may suggest freelancing or self-employment rather than working for a corporation or organisation. You may need to take some time off if you see the Hermit.

Card 10: The Wheel of Fortune

Element: Fire

Planet: Jupiter

Upright: Vocation, progress, revelation, good fortune, new phase, synchronicity

Reversed: Hurdles, disruptions, awful fate, unwelcome surprises

Card description: The Wheel of Fortune is an exceptionally symbolic tarot card, filled with numerous signs that each carry its own unique meaning. The primary feature of the card is a large wheel adorned with enigmatic symbols. There are four winged creatures, such as the angel, eagle, bull and lion, associated with the fixed zodiac signs of Aquarius, Scorpio, Taurus and Leo.

Each animal holds a set of books, symbolising the Torah and the knowledge and insight it imparts. The snake on the card represents the process of descending to Earth. Atop the wheel, a sphinx represents the wisdom of kings and gods, while at the centre, the rising figure of the devil or Anubis suggests a cycle of perpetual rise and fall.

The Egyptian symbols of the sphinx and Anubis, who represents the underworld, further reinforce the idea of a perpetual cycle. As one rises, the other falls, and vice versa, creating a balance of forces.

Number association: Number 10 sums up to number 1 when the digits are added. But, if we see the digits independently, we see that 10 comprises numbers 1 and 0. Number 1 represents the Magician and number 0 represents the Fool. Remember when I mentioned about the Fool that this card increases the worth of the one it appears next to? Similarly, the Wheel of Fortune has the hidden magical powers of the Magician along with the zeal, curiosity and enthusiasm of the Fool, making your luck turn towards either side.

Personal growth: This card symbolises the cyclic nature of life and suggests aligning yourself with the ebb and flow of the universe. Try not to exert too much control. Have faith that everything will work out as it should in the end.

About a person: This card could be someone who brings you good luck or helps you open doors. This person may unexpectedly appear to you, and the encounter be predestined.

Money: The economy is improving. Your financial situation should improve shortly, possibly due to a fortunate turn of events. Opportunities may present themselves simply by being in the right place at the right time.

Love: Your romantic life is going to get better. A new romance enters your life, or an existing connection improves. You don't need to do anything to attract the good fortune of the Wheel of Fortune. It just happens when the timing is right.

Career: There is a chance that you'll strike it rich. Good fortune appears unintentionally or in an unplanned manner. Without exerting effort, a complicated work scenario becomes easy, or events go in your favour.

Card 11: Justice

Astrological sign: Libra

Element: Air

Upright: Unbiased, togetherness, truce-maker, careful, proportionate, verity

Reversed: Incorrect, irresponsible, trickery, immature, preconception, shabbiness

Card description: The Justice card is among the tarot's most powerful symbols. It stands for justice, equity, and the rule of law. A woman holds scales in her left hand, which shows the need to weigh intuition alongside logic as she sits in her chair. A double-edged sword in her right hand is a symbol of objectivity. A square on her crown represents the sharp mind necessary for judging fairly. A purple cloak hangs behind her, and two grey pillars stand tall. The woman wears a red cloak and reveals a white shoe under it. It's a spiritual reminder that the results of their actions are what she brings to them.

Number association: Number 11 is known as a Master Number in numerology. It attracts tonnes of things towards itself. Number 1 in tarot represents the Magician. This means two 1's coming together are likely to multiply the Magician's strength. I feel number 11 is usually unpredictable. Such people may be filled with enormous energy at a particular point or behave like a dead battery at some other. They may oscillate between two extremes.

Personal growth: To become more kind, compassionate and unselfish, settle disagreements, correct wrongs, and alter your behaviour. In order to create balance in your life, you should try to accomplish it in all aspects. Consider the perspectives of others. To bring about peace and harmony, meditate on this card.

About a person: The Justice could be a lawyer, a judge, or legal figure. The card could also refer to someone who resolves conflicts, maintains peace, or ensures that things function smoothly. This individual is usually honest and fair-minded, with the ability to see other people's perspectives as well as their own.

Money: This card represents a just and equitable wealth distribution. If the money or property is yours but stuck in a legal tussle, Justice may indicate that whatever it may take, it will be determined in your favour. Retaliation may be required in specific instances. Obtain riches ethically and use them for the common good rather than for the advantage of a select few.

Love: There may be a need for a more equal system. You need to be fair, honest and considerate in a relationship. One of you may need to correct a mistake or change your conduct to restore balance and peace.

Career: Your workplace requires balance, justice and honesty. Equitable labour and responsibility distributions may be required. Justice can also refer to a point in time when issues have been addressed, and emotions have dissipated. It may represent a legal issue in some cases.

Card 12: The Hanged Man

Element: Water

Planet: Neptune/Ketu

Upright: Versatile, adaptable, reincarnation, free, saving

Reversed: Desire for material things, self-centred, lack of self-command, vulnerable in domination, calvary

Card description: The card shows a man dangling upside down from the tree of life by one foot. It is said that this tree, which has its origins far below ground, holds up the stars above. It's widely believed that the man on the gallows is hanging by his own choice. His calm expression lends credence to this theory. The branches have caught his right foot, but his left foot remains free. Concurrently, his hands are behind his back, forming an inverted triangle. He's wearing red pants, which stand for the body and human passion, and a blue shirt, which stands for knowledge. The yellow accents on his attire—including his shoes, hair, and halo—speak about his wit and wisdom.

Number association: Number 12 is strongly linked with the heaven above. It talks about the cosmic energy and situations that may appear to be incomplete, painful, troublesome or misleading but will ultimately settle. You will then be out of the chaos. 12 carries religious, spiritual, mythological and magical significance—12 months, 12 zodiacs, etc.

Personal growth: Allow yourself to let go of old, confining thoughts or behaviours in order to embrace new, more useful ones. To become more trusting and less controlling, meditate on this card.

About a person: The Hanged Man may appear to be someone who defies authority and marches to the beat of a different drummer. This person may be unconcerned about the physical environment. This card could also indicate someone in your life who acts as a catalyst for change.

Money: The Hanged Man is frequently associated with a sacrifice or a loss. You may need to cut your losses or give up something safe to go forward. This card may suggest that you abandon a materialistic way of life in order to pursue better principles. This card also says it's time to change if the way you've been doing things is no longer profitable.

Love: It is necessary to make a change. Give over the reins. For the sake of the partnership, you may have to set aside egoistic tendencies and desires. Alternatively, depending on the circumstances, you may be better off quitting a relationship that no longer serves you.

Career: It is time for a 180-degree pivot. Rather than following the usual path of action, you must drastically alter your behaviour: out with the old, in with the new. Perhaps it's time for you to hunt for a new job or leave a stable one for something challenging and gratifying.

Card 13: Death (Transformation)

Astrological sign: Scorpio

Element: Water

Upright: Transition, transparent, moulding, good end

Reversed: Unstable, unadaptable, missed favourable conditions, end of a friendship

Card description: The Death card shown the messenger of death riding in on a stunning white steed, waving a black flag with a white pattern. The messenger is a skeleton that survives long after everything else about the human body has decayed away. As a representation of Death's indestructibility, he garbs himself in armour. As Death cleanses all, the white horse he rides represents holiness. Below him, a king and a pauper lie side by side in the dirt to drive home the point that death does not care about social status, ethnicity, or sexual orientation.

Number association: 13 is the number that signifies change and uncertainty, as is said in the lotto—lucky for some and unlucky for some. It is not a dreadful number, though it may bring upon a change with some turbulence, pain or suffering. Better times are ahead, and you will be stronger.

Personal growth: You must let go of ideas, behaviours, a way of life, or individuals, who are impeding your development. It's time to let go of a part of yourself or an old way of life so that better things can emerge from the ashes. This card can assist you in a transition or loss by meditating on it.

About a person: Death represents someone who helps you transform, perhaps by assisting, in letting go of an old way of life and embracing a new one. It could also be a sign of someone leaving your life. This card could symbolise a person who works with death and regeneration, such as a building renovator, or a surgeon in some cases.

Money: The Death card can indicate the end of a job or a career path, as well as a significant change in your working position. Consider switching to something more challenging and gratifying if your job is too confining.

Love: If a relationship isn't satisfying you anymore, it's time to call it quits and look for a new one. The card may also urge you to alter your relationship with a spouse or a love partner, letting go of old attitudes and habits and replacing them with new ones that promote progress.

Career: The Death card can indicate the end of a job or a career path, as well as a significant change in your working position. Consider switching to something more challenging and gratifying if your current job is too confining.

Card 14: Temperance

Astrological sign: Sagittarius

Element: Fire

Upright: Concord, sacrifice, adjustable, calm, patience, physically fit

Reversed: Hot-headed, poor perception, a difference of opinion, clashes, discontented housemates

Card description: The Temperance card shows a winged angel with ambiguous gender. The angel is a symbol of harmony between the sexes. One of the feet of the angel is submerged in water, standing for the unconscious mind, while the other is planted firmly on solid ground, symbolising the external world. She wears a blue robe with a divine triangle enclosed in a square. This represents that humans are bound by the natural law and Earth. She's juggling two cups, each holding water symbolic of the conscious and unconscious minds. She pours water from one to another, representing unity and infinity.

This card, in every detail, symbolises equilibrium, the state of perfect harmony achieved through the complementary union of opposites. Before diving headfirst into something new, she suggests giving it a trial run.

Number association: Number 14 represents new beginnings and a positive change. It is a powerful compound number with the vibrations of number 1 (leadership/initiative), 4 (discipline/organised) and total summing to number 5 (change/growth). You may embrace cycles of good and bad together depending on how you channelise your energies. The balance would be the key to moving through what you are going through. But certainly, on a positive note—this card reassures you that the troubles will soon end, and you may be on the verge of entering something new.

Personal growth: You must moderate your conduct and avoid any excesses. Pursue a life that is more tranquil and balanced. Make a conscious effort to be more forgiving, kind and fair to others—and yourself. To relieve stress and restore equilibrium, meditate on this card.

About a person: Temperance can signify a peacemaker or a mediator; someone who works to reconcile conflicts and problems. This card can also represent someone balanced, empathetic, and at ease with themselves.

Money: Work and recreation must be balanced for your life to be complete. This card may also indicate the need to reconcile with employees, clients, or colleagues. In your workplace, distribute responsibilities evenly. Stay away from power disputes and don't get too ambitious.

Love: Allow love to unfold gently and calmly instead of having ego fights and power struggles. Now, more than ever, balance, acceptance and equality are crucial.

Career: Balance work and recreation for your life to be complete. This card may also indicate the need to reconcile with employees, clients, or colleagues. In your workplace, distribute responsibilities evenly. Stay away from power disputes and don't get too ambitious.

Card 15: The Devil

Astrological sign: Capricorn

Element: Earth

Upright: Addiction, obsession, oppression, playfulness

Reversed: Freedom, release, regaining control, independence

Card description: The Devil card shows Baphomet, a well-known satyr guise of the devil. The Devil is bat-winged and has an inverted pentagram on his forehead in addition to being half-goat and half-man. To demonstrate his superiority, he has a naked man and woman chained to a pedestal on which he stands.

When a human spends enough time with the devil, they lose some of their humanity and develops horns, just like the devil. There's an air of captivity about the chained figures that make it seem like the Devil has them in his power. The flames on the man's tail represents addiction to power, while the bowl of grapes on the woman's tail represents her desire for the finer things in life.

Neither the man nor the woman appears to be in a particularly cheerful mood. They no longer have any control over their lives and feel humiliated by their lack of autonomy.

Number association: Number 15 has mixed vibrations of numbers 1, 5 and 6. Number 15 sums up to number 6, representing Venus. The Devil card here also shows a man and woman being naked, which may refer to sexual intimacy situations. Number 15 usually represents an urge, expansion and deep desire/desperation to get something. On a positive note, it may represent creativity, entrepreneurial traits, etc., while on the negative side, it may represent a con artist, a dictator or a person with not-so-good intentions.

Personal growth: Thoughts, fears and powerful emotions may exert total control over you. It is good to spend time meditating on the Devil to learn about the various factors in your life that are causing you distress or to be released from an unhealthy attachment in your life.

About a person: To represent the concept of the Devil, you must possess the following characteristics: control, undermining, intimidation, and the exacerbation of negative traits. You can use this photo to capture a part of yourself that you don't normally show—to reflect your 'shadow side' or 'inner demons'.

Money: It is possible that you are too attached to money and possessions. Sometimes in the pursuit of wealth, you lose sight of other aspects that are important as well. Are you gaining an unfair advantage at someone else's expense? So, if this advice is correct, you should rethink your values.

Love: If someone has an obsession, a fixation, or a desire, they may not be able to see other people or situations with clarity. The Devil can also describe a destructive relationship or a partner who is not good for you, but who you stay with because you are unwilling for change. At the same time, it is not easy to discover which relationships meet that description.

Career: This card indicates you may be a working professional. In all likelihood, you've allowed your career to get in your way. Fear of change could be why you're not searching for a new job or starting a business. People who warn you that someone else is involved in questionable practices may not report it out of fear of retribution.

Card 16: The Tower

Element: Fire

Planet: Mars

Upright: Destruction, chaos, fickle, degraded, disturbed

Reversed: Talented, adaptable, manipulative

Card description: The Tower card depicts a tall tower perched atop a mountain. The tower is struck by lightning, starting a fire. People are jumping out of windows as flames burst through them, in an act of desperation. It's possible they represent the same chained figures seen in the Devil card. They're looking for a way out of the chaos and devastation they're experiencing on the inside. The Tower represents unrealistic goals that are based on fallacious reasoning. Destroying the tower is necessary to make way for a new era, as it will rid the world of the old ways. Inspiration or a realisation may come to you suddenly.

Number association: Number 16 often appears when a spiritual message is in store for you. Something that the universe wants you to learn and explore. Looking at the image on the card—we can say that these lessons are often not going to be easy, and you may be missing peace of mind. This card appears in a reading to bring back order, stability and structure in your life.

Personal growth: By demolishing the protective barriers you've constructed to keep yourself comfortable, the Tower shocks you into recognising how you've been deluding yourself. Rather than trying to hold on to illusory security, embrace the changes and freedom that occur. Meditating on the Tower can assist you in navigating a challenging transition.

About a person: In your life, the Tower represents someone who is an agent of change. They can appear out of nowhere and then vanish just as quickly. This person forces you to confront the truth and let go of your delusions.

Money: You may experience a significant change in your financial situation. This upheaval may strike without warning and result in the loss of money or property. However, when your false sense of security cracks, you may feel liberated from obligations and constraints.

Love: In a relationship, the Tower represents a split or transformation. Illusions about a spouse or you may be dispelled, allowing you to view things more clearly. Although this abrupt transition may be painful at first, the freedom that follows will be well worth it.

Career: Your job situation can take a turn for the worst. This upheaval could rock your foundations or jeopardise your belief in the need for change. It is necessary to demolish old structures in order to achieve greater independence and expressive freedom.

Card 17: The Star

Astrological sign: Aquarius

Element: Air

Upright: Optimistic, humble, physically fit, free from stress, turn dreams into reality

Reversed: Negativity, bilk, arrogant, distrust, lack of confidence

Card description: The card shows a woman kneeling at the edge of a small pond. She holds two bottles of water in her hands. She empties the contents of one onto the dry land as if to give it life and ensure its fertility. The verdant landscape around her shows that her efforts are paying off. She empties the other in five rivulets, indicating the five senses. The fact that the woman is able to put one foot into the water demonstrates her spiritual prowess and resolve. She has displayed her practical strengths and abilities by keeping one foot firmly on the ground. The seven rays of light, that make up the chakras are depicted as stars behind her. A bird perched on the branch of a tree is the sacred ibis of wisdom. According to astrology, The Star is associated with the sign of Aquarius.

Number association: Number 17 holds a special message for us. It says to let go of what is holding you back—what is it? A situation, a person, a thought, a limiting belief? Something is making you feel stuck in a place and is not letting you grow or progress. As per Vedic numerology, the number 8 represents Saturn which brings with it certain challenges, obstructions, delays and struggles, unlike the other schools of numerology that consider it auspicious. Remember, the atomic number of oxygen is also 8, and oxygen is the basic requirement for the survival of an individual. Thus this card would hold importance in a reading whenever you encounter this.

Personal growth: Don't give up your values, says the Star. Even your craziest aspirations are possible for you to achieve. If you're feeling down in the dumps or facing difficulties in life, focus on this card to boost your self-esteem.

About a person: The Star might signify someone with a 'star' quality and draws attention to himself or herself wherever they go. A relationship with this person could help you be in the spotlight or increase your chances of success.

Money: Be optimistic. Your wishes may come true. The Star is one of the most promising cards, and an improvement in your financial status may be linked to your employment situation. You worked hard to achieve your goals and will get rewards for your efforts.

Love: Your happy aspirations are going to become a reality. Even though you may still need to work on creating or refining a relationship, The Star advises you to be optimistic.

Career: You could become a 'star' in your field of work or expertise soon. Now is the time to put in the effort necessary to achieve your goals. Keep your ideals in mind and work hard to achieve them. It is possible to overcome obstacles. It's only a matter of time before you succeed.

Card 18: The Moon

Astrological sign: Pisces

Element: Water

Upright: Perceptive, plenty of chances, enlightened

Reversed: Baffling, emotional, disguise, false, mystery for others

Card description: The moon shows a full moon, a symbol of dreams and intuition A wolf and a dog, representing our animalistic nature, stand on opposite sides of a path, with the former being domesticated and the latter wild and savage. A crawfish is crawling up the path from a pond, showing the unfolding of consciousness. Two towers stand in the background, one on each side of the central path, alluding to the doubles in this card's design. The card seems to suggest a choice between two outcomes. As we make our way down the path, we straddle the divide between our rational, civilised selves and the more primal, wild parts of ourselves, symbolised by the dog and the wolf, respectively.

The towers at either end represent good and evil, and the fact that they look similar may be interpreted as a metaphor for our inability to tell them apart.

Number association: Number 18 is powerful in numerology. It carries the vibrations of numbers 1, 8 and 9 and signals towards new beginnings and abundance. If this card keeps repeating in a reading, it signifies success. Broadly, it guides you to keep going and gives you confidence that you are on the right track.

Personal growth: Contact your subconscious and address any anxieties, blocks, memories, or hidden concerns. Use this card to connect with your hidden side or to ignite your imagination.

About a person: The Moon could be a symbol for an artist or someone very creative. It can also refer to someone who is troubled by psychological or hidden concerns. This individual has the potential to awaken your dark side, delve into your secrets, or have a profound impact on you.

Money: There may be hidden conditions in some aspects of a financial matter that are obscure. Now is not the time to become involved in risky investments or transactions. It's possible to experience financial ups and downs. The Moon may represent making money through artistic efforts, for those who are artistically inclined.

Love: Between two people, there is a profound, ideal bond. Others may be perplexed by your attraction, and you may be unable to articulate why. This card can sometimes represent a secret relationship. It could also signal a tumultuous relationship with numerous emotional highs and lows.

Career: Examine a job situation or a career decision in greater detail. Certain secrets may be revealed soon. It is also possible that a situation is in flux. Maybe you have unrealistic expectations about your job or need to be more realistic about your talents. In your work, the Moon may advise you to be more imaginative.

Card 19: The Sun

Element: Fire

Planet: Sun

Season: Summer

Upright: Cheer, contentment, attraction, energetic, renown, nirvana

Reversed: Bad decisions, lack of clarity, pique, turmoil

Card description: The Sun card shows joy and contentment. A sun shines brightly in the sky. The dawn depicted on this card comes after the darkest of nights. Our planet's life depends on the sun, a symbol of the vitality of life. A child is depicted in the foreground, engaged in happy play. The child represents joy from being at one with one's authentic self. Clothed only in skin and bones, the child has nothing to hide. The card also evokes the pristine purity of a child's heart. The horse the kid is riding is white. The horse is also a symbol of power and strength in this context.

Number association: Number 19 keeps you young and allows you to think with a fresh perspective. You exhibit briskness and strength. You like pleasures, but you have to be cautious as well. This number encourages you to dream big and achieve your goals.

Personal growth: The Sun inspires you to be joyful and share your happiness with others. Take charge of your life's circumstances and make the most of it. Meditate on this card to boost your self-esteem or to find clarity on a problem.

About a person: The Sun represents a capable, self-assured individual who leads by example. They are someone you should respect as a beneficial force in your life. This person could be a leader, a visionary, or someone who assists you in seeing things more clearly.

Money: The days are getting brighter. Financial issues disappear, confusion clears, and you see how to maximise your resources. This card suggests that you should make investments or start a business.

Love: This card represents happiness, openness, and a close relationship between two people. You have something special in common and can bring out the best in one another. Thanks to the great light of the Sun, You can easily see each other and your relationship in a new light.

Career: You are in command and are making the most of your powers. You clearly understand what you want to accomplish and how to get there. You are likely to experience success, accolades, and recognition. You can also inspire others and assist them with their efforts.

Card 20: Judgement

Element: Fire

Planet: Pluto

Upright: Happiness, reincarnation, reap rich dividends, remission, talented

Reversed: Stubborn, dread, detain, feeling of deep regret

Card description: The Judgement card shows the many forms that the final judgement takes in different mythologies. Women, men, and children are rising from the grave in response to the trumpet call of Archangel Gabriel. Their arms are outstretched as if inviting the universe to pass judgement on them. They are about to face God, have their works evaluated, and learn whether or not they will spend the rest of eternity in heaven or hell. Judgement is inevitable and will be final, as symbolised by the enormous tidal wave in the background.

The ruler of the underworld, Pluto, also rules judgement. Death, which also serves as a reminder that all things must eventually come to an end before a new beginning can begin, carries overtones of this card.

Number association: Number 20 usually promises balance and harmony after seeing a period of turbulence. You may be entering your spiritual journey and connecting with your higher self. Most of the time, if it appears with positive cards—it represents progress, new opportunities and experiences. It may indicate a time of transition, change or growth—so do not be afraid of taking a risk.

Personal growth: In your own development, judgement denotes a period of transition and the end of a cycle. Before deciding what to do in the future, assess your behaviours, beliefs and progress. Meditation on this card may help you decide which course to choose if a substantial shift is required.

About a person: This card could represent a judge, elected official, or any other figure of authority, who has the power to pronounce judgement or make decisions for others. It could also indicate a person who acts as a catalyst for change.

Money: In a financial matter, you must decide. This option has the potential to divert you from your current course and alter your life. Your choice will have an impact, not just on your current financial circumstances but also on your future finances.

Love: You are standing at a crossroads in a relationship and need to make a choice. There may be concerns about authority, ethics and honesty. Consider your options carefully because they may have a significant impact on your current relationship as well as future relationships.

Career: It is vital to make a decision on your employment or career path. It may be time to switch jobs or pursue an entirely different career path. Choose carefully, because what you do now will have long-term and far-reaching consequences.

Card 21: The World

Element: Earth

Planet: Saturn

Upright: Consummate, culmination, rejoice, win accolades, complete package

Reversed: Instability, fickle-mindedness, restlessness, postponing things

Card description: The World card shows a dancing woman. The woman has one leg crossed over the other and holds wands in both. She is a representation of harmony and development in physical expression. Her embodiment of wholeness and completion is not static but dynamic and eternal.

A green laurel wreath, representing success, surrounds the woman, while a red ribbon wrapped around the wreath represents infinity. The four corners of the card feature the same four figures (angel, bull, lion and eagle) in the Wheel of Fortune. The four figures represent the zodiac signs of Scorpio, Leo, Aquarius and Taurus, which in turn are symbolic of the four cardinal directions, the four classical elements, and the four evangelists. Together, they represent the balance of all their powers.

Number association: Number 21 represents faith—in yourself, your abilities, or the eternal energy that controls us. This number exuberates confidence. Just because this is the last number in the Major Arcana series—it may refer to the delay or things coming with a delay. Although the surrounding cards around this would be able to decide whether this card leads to the delay or the delay is about to get closure now.

Personal growth: You have absorbed all the lessons in life to this point, and you are right on track with your growth. Continue to expand steadily and slowly. At the moment, everything is fine in the world.

About a person: The World could represent someone who doesn't have to work hard to be happy or successful. This person cooperates with rather than opposes the forces of the universe. This person makes modest, steady advancement in life by wisely utilising their skills.

Money: Everything is as it should be in terms of financial matters. Don't rush an investment or a financial venture. It is critical to be meticulous. You'll get what you've worked hard for.

Love: Slowly but steadily, a relationship develops. Relax, and don't try to force anything to happen sooner than it should. This relationship incorporates all that you have learnt about love so far. This card represents emotional maturity as well as a sense of fulfilment. It can also depict a relationship progressing from a personal to a spiritual level.

Career: You can accomplish your objectives because they are timely. Even though everything appears to be taking longer than you expected, everything is proceeding according to plan. To obtain a positive outcome, pay close attention to details and apply what you have learnt in the past.

❑

CHAPTER 3

The Minor Arcana

That brings us to the end of the first leg, i.e., The Major Arcana. I hope you find it interesting and exciting to learn. Now we will move further to explore the next leg, i.e., The Minor Arcana.

These comprise Wands, Cups, Swords and Pentacles (Coins).

The Minor Arcana refers to routine activities. These cards are practical and have a temporary influence. They act as a report card of routine activities and their remedies if something goes wrong.

In totality, there are 56 ways (cards) of analysing your capabilities.

Suit of Wands

Wands, Rods or Batons are the names given to the first category of Minor Arcana.

Surprises into shocks, construction into destruction, deactivation into activation and vice versa is the power of fire, the element related to this category or suit.

It makes you not think not only big and long-term but also implement your ploy to accomplish your all-time goals. It empowers you to convert your virtual and illusionary world into reality. These cards cover the four domains such as occupation, employment, endeavour and aim.

If commitment, triumph, and rage are the booming features attached to this set, then on the contrary, careless acts, despair and dissatisfaction are some of its banal features.

It is clear till now that the stretching capability or the limits of these 78 cards are endless. The expressive powers of these cards are not feasible to explore within some time, but sometimes the whole life is needed as more and more advancement is going on. So here, it's not possible to portray all the information. We will instead focus on the crucial ones.

It is time to move your hands towards the deck of cards and take out Wands numbered 1 to 10 and place the remaining cards in the deck.

The route is the same that you followed for Major Arcana. Make a pile of cards, draw the first card, i.e., Ace of Wands, and spend some time with it. Try to gather all the thoughts that come to your mind—bright or dull. Make notes of all in your diary. Thoroughly try to solve its enigmatic nature. Try this activity with all the cards, one by one.

A lot depends on which type of deck you are using. Different decks have different ways of portraying the information. Try to memorise the details on the cards and if not, then examine the card carefully and try to link some positive and negative words with them. The human mind is more susceptible to analysing pictures or diagrams when compared to words and numbers.

The encoding scheme that you do on your own is the best activity to trace. It will help to open your mind and grab the upcoming tedious task in the form of spreads.

Ace of Wands

Element: Fire

Astrological signs: Aries, Leo, Sagittarius

Upright: Artistic, fresh, productive, new horizons

Reversed: Irritation, avarice, boredom

Card description: The suit of Wands represents the element of fire, and the Ace of Wands is the card most closely associated with fire in the deck. On the card, a hand emerges from a cloud, wand in hand.

When we examine this card, we see a hand holding a wand extending from a cloud. The fact that some of the leaves of the wand have sprouted is supposed to stand for harmony and advancement on both the spiritual and material levels. A castle can be seen in the distance, and it represents the various opportunities that will be available in the years to come.

Number association: If your readings contain a lot of aces, you'll know when something new with a lot of potential is coming. They are merely formless pure energy, and it is up to you to mould them and materialise the potential they stand for. They are unstable because they are raw. They can overwhelm you very soon if you don't take care.

Personal growth: The Ace represents a period of fresh experiences and opportunities for development. Your creative energy is reawakening, as is your self-assurance. Open oneself up to new challenges and chances with delight.

About a person: The Ace of Wands, as a person, is someone who exemplifies attributes such as perseverance, drive and success in their everyday life. These folks are always looking out for fresh concepts and aren't hesitant to take chances to accomplish what they set out to do. They have a robust sense of individualism, which can often cause them to come across as pretentious or overly concerned with themselves. As a result, it is essential for them to maintain their connection to their spirituality to remind themselves that success is not the only indicator of their value.

Money: The Ace indicates an early commitment to a creative project. You may begin your venture. Make money doing what you love. Look for new experiences and chances. Have faith in yourself and think outside the box when the matter is related to money.

Love: This card frequently denotes the start of a new passionate relationship or a surge of zeal in an existing one. Your imagination and creativity could be sparked by a relationship. Act on your feelings. Do not wait for the other one to initiate contact. A lover will very likely respond positively.

Career: It's possible that you'll be presented with an opportunity that allows you to use your imagination and talents. Now is the perfect time to invest your heart and soul into a project, career, or business enterprise. Take benefit out of new opportunities that come across. Success is achievable, but you must be prepared to put forth the effort required to get it. Optimism and self-confidence are key assets.

Two of Wands

Element: Fire

Astrological signs: Aries, Leo, Sagittarius

Upright: New venture, glory comes to you, planning, potential

Reversed: Aimless, good-for-nothing, disappointment, hesitation

Card description: The Two of Wands card shows a man standing in a castle. He is holding a small globe in his right hand. The man has a bird's-eye view of the vast landscape below him. To the left of the man is an ocean, and to the right is a land mass that extends for a considerable distance. The man wears an orange tunic and red hat, symbolising his exuberance toward life in general and his yearning for excitement. The globe he holds in his hand represents the possibilities that lie ahead for him for expanding his horizons to include more aspects of life.

Number association: The topic of the twos is pairing up, with all the complications that this union entails. We go from the oneness, and the twos offer a glimpse of togetherness. The twos typically stand for harmony and the coming together of opposing elements to form a whole. This harmony can occasionally be so flawless that it makes it impossible to move on and causes paralysis when a decision needs to be made.

Personal growth: Define your objectives, ideals, territories, or missions in detail. Don't just sit, relax and observe life go by. Instead, be involved. To make your dreams come true, this is the best time to utilise your willpower.

About a person: The Two of Wands, as a person, is a born leader and possesses an alluring charisma that compels others to follow in their footsteps. They have a concrete plan for their future and are committed to putting in the effort necessary to make it a reality. They can be successful because of their bravery and competitive nature but have to be careful that their drive to be successful does not negatively affect other elements of their life.

Money: You must take complete control of your finances. Learn the ways to manage them effectively. Don't be scared. Even if you choose to accept someone else's help, don't put your self-worth, principles, or control at risk, by doing so.

Love: The number 2 represents the point in the development of a relationship when both partners must announce themselves and begin forming the partnership. You may create a rewarding partnership with vision and excitement. This card can also represent a collaborative effort in which each partner is inspired by the other.

Career: Put your body and spirit into what you are pursuing. It's now time to carry out your plans. Take charge of your professional circumstances and pursue your goals zealously—don't let anything get in the way. Rather than settling for comfort, ease and security, seek out challenges that will push your abilities.

Three of Wands

Element: Fire

Astrological signs: Aries, Leo, Sagittarius

Upright: A vista of domains, dedication, alliance

Reversed: Egoistic, careless, thwarting

Card description: The Three of Wands card shows a man standing on the edge of a cliff, gazing out over the water and the surrounding mountains. From his position, he has a clear view of everything that lies in his path including challenges and opportunities. The wands are driven into the ground around the man who holds one of them in his hand. He appears to be anticipating the future and thinking about the level of dedication he has for his plans, as well as the strategy he will use to put those plans into action and make them a reality.

Number association: The tarot's threes are governed by group dynamics, and they represent many events that might happen when groups of people or ideas join. It also denotes an initial completion of a first phase of some kind because it is also conceptualised symbolically as completion (the first polygon, the Holy Trinity, etc.).

Personal growth: The number 3 denotes a period of intense personal commitment. Your creativity and inspiration have been resurrected. Invest time in refining your concepts. Whatever you put your body and spirit into will bring you joy and inspire others.

About a person: The Three of Wands, as a person, is one who is resolute in pursuit of their dreams and has a wealth of ambitious plans and schemes. Their confidence is matched only by their determination and persistence. They will let nothing stand in the way of achieving their lofty objectives. Their unbounded optimism might make them appear overly competitive and arrogant, which turns off other people. It is essential for them to maintain a healthy balance between their ambition and humility.

Money: In order to enhance revenues, publicise yourself and promote your activities. Take command, be energetic, and make it happen. You can inspire others with your passion and confidence, which can help a financial transaction succeed.

Love: It's time to show love genuinely, openly and passionately. Make it crystal clear to your partner that you are concerned. Cherish your love and affection. This card may represent marriage or another type of commitment that recognises and celebrates your partnership in some instances.

Career: Make a sincere, enthusiastic effort to express your creativity. This can be an exciting time when you have put a lot of creative work into a project and your abilities noticed. To be successful, you might need to adapt to others. It's crucial to have integrity.

Four of Wands

Element: Fire

Astrological signs: Aries, Leo, Sagittarius

Upright: Gratification, new abode, conclusion

Reversed: Degenerate, discourteous act, short-tempered

Card description: The Four of Wands shows a couple dancing beneath a beautiful wreath suspended between four crystal-tipped wands. The floral arch seems to represent a traditional wedding ceremony. The couple are celebrating with flowers in their hands. The picture evokes feelings of fulfilment and satisfaction from achieving one's goals.

Number association: The number four typically denotes a strong foundation and reliability for oneself and others. The goal here is to grow and evolve since, even if the foundation has been laid there may occasionally be some disappointment because things may not have exactly as planned. The fours indicate that the universe is encouraging us to advance and flourish.

Personal growth: The Four of Wands represents a time of calm, contentment, and comfort. You feel excellent not only about yourself but also about your place in the world. This is because you are aware that you've earned it. Let others also know about your life experiences.

About a person: The Four of Wands, as a person, exudes joy and enthusiasm and is often the one who brings people together. They enjoy planning parties and staying in touch with loved ones. However, their cheerful demeanour can sometimes become a burden when they feel obliged to fake happiness. This may lead them to suppress negative emotions like anger or sadness, but they need to remember that it's okay to experience negative emotions as well.

Money: If you get this card, you will have financial security and ease. The four implies that an investment, company, or other financial concern should go well for you. It's time to start reaping the benefits you deserve.

Love: In a partnership, the Four of Wands represents joy, stability and harmony. It is now easy to sort out the previous concerns, as romance is in the air. You may attract someone suitable for you since you know what you want and are confident.

Career: After a period of hard work, success and happiness come. A project or job started right now is likely to provide you with happiness and satisfaction. It's time to pay close attention to the finer points. Also, make sure that you follow them. This card can also represent the completion of a project and the happiness that comes with it.

Five of Wands

Element: Fire

Astrological signs: Aries, Leo, Sagittarius

Upright: Sacrifice, intellect, contradiction

Reversed: Deceit, churlish tricks, bad behaviour

Card description: Five men, each with a wand in hand, raise them high in the air to represent the Five of Wands. As is usually the case with the tarot card number five, the querent may have to deal with conflict/change. The card indicates a tension between the men or a sign that they are simply enjoying the thrill of competing against one another and that any ill will between them is merely friendly rivalry.

The casualness with whichh they hold their wands suggests that this is more a theatrical than an actual battle. Each of the men wear different outfits suggesting that they have different belief systems and are not in harmony.

Number association: The fives stand for transition, change, turbulence, and strife (at times). The fives come after the fours and amplify the same energy. The fives encourage us to seek within for a deeper cause for why to move forward when that energy explodes. We must advance to overcome this instability and move forward.

Personal growth: Set aside ego conflicts. Also, keep ingrained habits at bay as they prevent you from progressing. This card can also imply that your head is in the clouds and that you must deal with 'real world' issues.

About a person: The Five of Wands, as a person, is seeking who they are and who they want to be. They could be having trouble finding significance in their life. They frequently have low self-esteem and question their capacity to achieve the goals they set for themselves. Despite this, they are still caring and sympathetic people who want to stand out and be distinctive but are afraid of what others will think of them because of it. They might be able to improve their self-esteem and discover genuine satisfaction after they acknowledge that their desires and requirements have merit.

Money: Resources, property, ideas, rights and territory are all areas where disagreements develop. There may be misunderstandings or arguments on ways to earn, spend or invest money. Be practical. You may lose money if you don't pay attention to what's going on around you. If so, don't seek financial counsel from others or initiate a court case concerning money or property.

Love: Squabbles between you and your partner are caused by minor issues. There is an eruption in ego-related fights, but there will be no resolution. Both of you are likely to be selfish, clinging to your beliefs and refusing to see the other person's point of view. Try to be more cooperative and adaptable.

Career: Arguments, ambiguity and disorder wreak havoc on your workplace or professional path. Progress is hampered by egotism and obstinacy. Perhaps you are overly idealistic and overlook practical or financial issues to your detriment.

Six of Wands

Element: Fire

Astrological signs: Aries, Leo, Sagittarius

Upright: Triumph, satisfaction, important events

Reversed: Despair, corrupt mind, late arrival

Card description: The Six of Wands shows a man wearing a victory wreath on his head. He is galloping through a sea of cheering supporters on horseback. White horses are commonly associated with virtue, power and prosperity. The supporter turnout shows the public's admiration for the rider's accomplishments. The man is trying to further emphasise his success by carrying a wand that has a wreath tied to it. The man seems proud of his achievements rather than embarrassed by all the attention. The people around him respond with happiness and enthusiasm to this.

Number association: The sixes in contrast to the fives that indicate conflict, symbolise the transition from that conflict into a resolution, whether it is internal or external, whether it includes reconciliation or letting go. They represent the triumph over adversity and the dawning of light.

Personal growth: This is a time of excitement and achievement. You have been tested and risen to the occasion. Victory is yours. The Six of Wands can also represent the healing process, after a disease or accident. To bring success and pleasure to your life, meditate on this card.

About a person: The Six of Wands, as a person, is a highly competent and self-assured individual who exudes natural leadership qualities. They are well organised, focused on achieving their goals and use their charisma to motivate and influence those around them. They are upbeat, pleasant and enthusiastic people who enjoy being the centre of attention. But their self-assurance can occasionally take the form of arrogance, and they may require the support of their friends to avoid falling into this trap. They should also take care to avoid using the support of their followers or fans as a shield against the consequences of their actions.

Money: After a period of hard effort or struggle, success and financial benefits may finally be yours. This card represents success in legal and business matters. An investment, especially one that is long-term or involves some risk, should pay off.

Love: The number six denotes a period of joy, peace and collaboration. You and a partner work together to conquer obstacles and have fun. You are ready to express your feelings publicly and passionately, perhaps through marriage or a committed relationship. If you are looking for love, now is the time.

Career: Your work brings you success and enjoyment. Getting this card could indicate that you will triumph, obtain the right job, or flourish in a difficult task. The time to act and progress has arrived. You are rewarded for your efforts and given the recognition you deserve.

Seven of Wands

Element: Fire

Astrological signs: Aries, Leo, Sagittarius

Upright: Brave, shining star, stimulating

Reversed: Lack of confidence, poor management, lose chances

Card description: The Seven of Wands depicts a man facing off against his adversaries from a vantage point on the top of a hill. Below him, his rivals are posing a challenge. It appears he is defending this position while simultaneously attacking in retaliation. Interestingly, the man in the Rider Waite illustration of the Seven of Wands is wearing mismatched shoes. This could mean he is on shaky ground or without a firm opinion.

Number association: When there is a seven in a reading, it typically means that it's time to take a step back and reflect. The sevens challenge us to rethink and assess whether the course we are on, is the best one for us. Although it can occasionally feel lonely, this phase is necessary if you want to go forward with your true desires.

Personal growth: The Seven of Wands represents the development that comes through hard work, dedication and patience. You must show willingness to put in the effort to achieve your goals. Dispel negative attitudes and avoid those who bring you down.

About a person: The Seven of Wands, as a person, is someone who embodies the qualities of courage and is unafraid to fight for what they believe in, even in the face of opposition. They can be tremendous allies to marginalised people in their battle against injustice because of their strong convictions. On the other hand, they could be unduly defensive and accusing, seeing prejudice and unfair treatment where there is none. They need to have a more open mindset and be willing to offer the benefit of doubt to those around them.

Money: Even if things appear challenging now, stick with a financial enterprise, goal, or course of action. It's possible that you will have to put in a lot of effort to make a profit. Keep your cool. Don't get into a fight over money or property right now.

Love: You should make all the required adjustments to ensure the connection works. You can fix problems, but it will require time and effort. Don't give up on your dreams. Keep an optimistic approach even if it looks easy to give up.

Career: You should maintain excitement and work hard to attain your objectives. Set priorities and focus your efforts where they will have the greatest impact. Persevere; success is possible, but it will take time. Allow no disappointments, other people, or distractions to prevent you from achieving your goal.

Eight of Wands

Element: Fire

Astrological signs: Aries, Leo, Sagittarius

Upright: Energetic, journey, charge up

Reversed: Postpone, lack of thought, bad choices

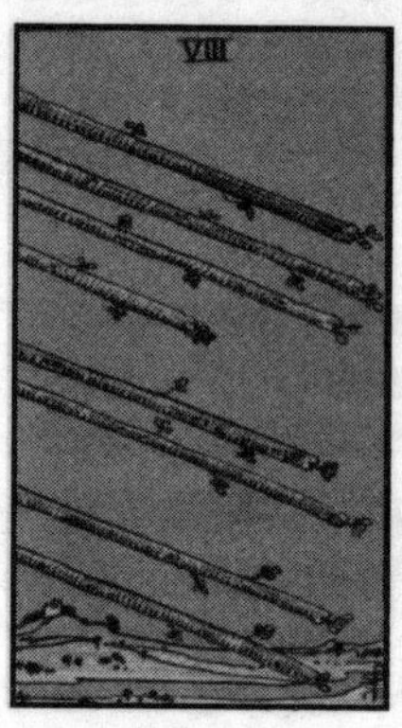

Card description: The image associated with the Eight of Wands is that of eight flying staves that give the impression that they are floating in the air. Some people might consider them to be blossoming wands that are moving at high speed. A blue sky serves as the backdrop for the area they are travelling through, which is meant to convey the idea there is little to no chance of anything getting in the way of these people reaching their final destination. It depicts a magnificent landscape, complete with a flowing river, the water giving the image a sense of motion and vitality. In addition, it seems as though the wands are about to touch down, which indicates the conclusion of a protracted journey.

Number association: The eights signify the end of a second phase and typically represent some form of accomplishment, whether it is materialistic or emotional. Here, growth may be in both directions, and it occasionally manifests itself in ways we least expect.

Personal growth: It is time to act right now. Put yourself out there, take some chances, and do something new that you have always wanted to try. Pursue what brings you joy.

About a person: The Eight of Wands, as a person, is someone with high motivation, a clear sense of goals, and no fear of change. They may have a great desire to travel and experience the world. They can frighten some people with their quick speed of life, yet they add excitement to others' lives. They are challenging to follow due to their relentless demeanour, yet it is in their character not to compromise their objectives for others. Such an individual will succeed in fast-paced and ruthless work and thrive in a competitive, academic or professional atmosphere. They excel at balancing obligations and multitasking.

Money: The number eight portends a period of frantic activity and rapid change. Quick thinking and decisive action may be required. Have faith that better chances, details, or outcomes are on the horizon. Seize the day!

Love: This card conveys ardour and exuberance. A brand-new romantic affair could start out of nowhere and take you by storm, or the sparks could reignite an old romantic relationship. When drawn, the Eight of Wands can sometimes indicate a sign of impulsive behaviour, such as a whirlwind marriage.

Career: You go through a hectic period in which new developments in the situation require you to think, move, and make choices hurriedly. You experience feelings of being both challenged and inspired during this time period. You can make significant headway right now, and the pace of your career could pick up. There is potential to travel for business.

Nine of Wands

Element: Fire

Astrological signs: Aries, Leo, Sagittarius

Upright: Confident, disciplined, persistence

Reversed: Adamant, mistrust, giving up

Card description: The Nine of Wands depicts a frail-looking man clinging to a wand while eight additional wands stand upright behind him. The man appears to be hurt but is still prepared to engage in another conflict and has a strong desire to prevail. He exudes an air of optimism and unyielding resolve, which both ought to serve him well as he faces off in this final conflict. This card depicts varied emotions, including hope, triumph and challenges.

Number association: The nines suggest close to completion, which could mean reaching a plateau. What appears to be the finish line might be a temporary stage. Even though there is a sense of finality, this is typically just a brief period before the cycle's conclusion.

Personal growth: Your problems are no longer an issue. You have faced and overcome obstacles, and as a result, you are much stronger. This card can also demonstrate recovery following sickness or injury.

About a person: The Nine of Wands, as a person, is someone with boundless potential to fulfil their ambitions. When seemingly faced with insurmountable obstacles, they persevere until they have achieved their goal, which is when their strengths are most evident. They benefit from having this trait since, in the end, they always get what they want.

They are focused and dedicated. They are so accustomed to success that they anticipate the same results from their next of kin. If they feel their children aren't working hard enough, they may even force their methods on them. As a result, they need to be reminded frequently to adopt a gentle parenting style and respect the decisions of others.

Money: The Nine of Wands represents financial stability and security. If you have had losses in the past, this card indicates that you are on the mend. However, it may take some time until you reach a position of unassailable strength and your assets reach their pinnacle. Keep on; you are in a solid position and can withstand adversity.

Love: The Nine of Wands, the 'silver lining' card, foreshadows happy days in the future. It could imply that you and a partner will resolve your problems or that if the relationship fails, you will be stronger. The nine may also tell you to wait for results rather than expecting them immediately.

Career: You are resilient. This quality will make you bounce back from setbacks. Even if you are disheartened, keep working towards your goal because the worst is over. Success and safety are on the horizon. Temporary pauses allow you to enhance your position. Hold your ground in the hardship period.

Ten of Wands

Element: Fire

Astrological signs: Aries, Leo, Sagittarius

Upright: Coerce, loyal, duty

Reversed: Cheat, profound language, stress

Card description: In this scene, a man is making his way towards a nearby town while carrying a heavy load of wood in the form of ten bundles of wands. The figure depicted in the Ten of Wands has overcome great adversity and is now bringing the fruits of his labour to their final destination. Even though he has not yet reached his final destination, he has made it through the most gruelling part of his journey and is ready to unwind and celebrate his accomplishment.

Number association: In the tens, we see the actual end of the cycle, that something has come full circle; this denotes that moving forward, we can head towards a fresh start.

Personal growth: The Ten of Wands is a fatigue card. You have taken on too much and need to take some time off. If that is not an option, find a strategy to increase your capacity to handle the responsibilities or duties assigned to you.

About a person: The Ten of Wands, as a person, is talented and diligent yet prone to self-punishment and overwork. Almost invariably, this individual will decide to prioritise others' needs over their own. While they may think they are just being kind, they are simply too terrified to take care of their own needs. They get exhausted and neglected because of always bearing other people's burdens. Such individuals should be aware of their requirements even though their kind and helpful disposition undoubtedly has benefits. They won't reach their full potential until they practise self-love and demand respect from others.

Money: Financial concerns may be weighing you down. You must continue to bear the burden because other people rely on you for support or because your financial status affects others. Number 10 might also indicate that you are overly concerned with money and need to broaden your horizons.

Love: Number 10 denotes a mature and responsible approach to relationships. You value love and have a strong bond with your lover. This card can sometimes represent marriage or a strong, long-lasting bond between two people who genuinely care for each other. It can also indicate a connection requiring a lot of time and effort.

Career: You have taken on more responsibilities or work than you are used to. You are tired of being burdened, yet you can't ignore your responsibilities, perhaps because others rely on you. To reduce stress, try delegating responsibilities and authority. Even though the obstacles you are facing are exhausting, they will force you to learn and become stronger.

Page of Wands

Element: Fire

Astrological signs: Aries, Leo, Sagittarius

Upright: Diligent, passionate, truehearted

Reversed: over-smart, hot-headed, destroyer

Card description: On a desolate landscape, a young man in fine clothes brazenly holds a stick while standing there. His shirt is emblazoned with salamanders and is intended to convey the idea that one can change from evil to good. This young man is a fervent advocate of spreading ideas of spiritual and social advancement that are beneficial to his fellow man. He does this with a lot of passion. The desert in the background conveys that he lives in a world that has not yet begun to bear fruit, and he is associated with the element of fire. As a result, his ideas are entirely based on conjecture. However, if he decided to use them and embark on the journey of his suit, his honesty of heart would lead him to achieve better fortunes.

Possible events: Spreading charisma, prevention is better than cure, gather all the information before dwelling on any project. Fate will take two childhood friends together, time to rejoice.

Personal growth: It will be good if you attend to practical things and keep track of all the minutiae of your life. You may be called upon to help others or to carry out a mission. The card expressly states that now is the time to pay attention to your health.

About a person: The Page of Wands is a person driven by their passions, is self-reliant and enjoys taking chances. They enjoy experiencing new things and looking for exciting opportunities. They take many trips a year to exotic locations and participate in varied social events where they meet new people. They have a childlike quality that makes them naturally upbeat and joyful. They are prepared to look past the shortcomings of others and usually miss the warning indications that something potentially harmful is about to happen.

Money: The Page of Wands is a card that represents transformation. It may advise you to sell an investment, property, business, or other financial asset and move on to a better opportunity. This card can also represent an unhealthy attachment to money and goods. Be brave; your fear of danger and change may restrict your success.

Love: This card shows a straightforward approach as well as a down-to-earth approach to a relationship. The card reflects the partner's description, which is less romantic and exciting and focuses on realistic or ordinary matters.

Career: This card represents working in a practical profession or a support role and could be a health-related topic or attribute. It could also be a sign of an entry-level job or training. Your work provides financial security but is lacking in zest and vibrancy. In comparison to self-expression or popularity, stability and money are more significant.

Knight of Wands

Element: Fire

Astrological signs: Aries, Leo, Sagittarius

Upright: Sporty, irregular, energetic

Reversed: Envious, wild, quarrelsome

Card description: The Knight of Wands rides a rearing horse, primed for battle. The outfit, including the horse, suggests the knight is ready for whatever lies ahead. The knight is in armour. He also sports a red plume on his armoured helmet. He looks ready for battle, though his large wand stands in for a sword. The mane on his orange horse makes it look like it is on fire. The intent to succeed in his mission is written all over the face of the Knight of Wands. Fire in a dominating factor in the symbolism of the Knight of Wands. The mane of his horse and the tassels at his wrists and shoulders are both fiery-red. In addition, he dons a yellow shirt having a symbol of a fiery salamander printed on it.

Possible events: Be ready to board the flight to some over-the-seas destination, revolutionary time.

Personal growth: This is the time to take care of physical and routine essentials. In all aspects of life, now is the time to be practical, compassionate, patient, honest and dependable. Helping others is the best approach to attain both personal and professional progress.

About a person: The Knight of Wands, as a person, is a charming and assured individual. The person depicted by this card never backs down from a challenge and does not hesitate to act because they are supremely self-confident. It is challenging to ignore their allure because they are passionate and just a touch rebellious. A person would not want to escape the influence of their personality once they are in it. Being around these people causes others to emulate them and exhibit their boldness, spontaneity, and confidence.

Money: Money will come your way as a result of your great labour and sensible investment. This card can also imply property in specific cases. You must avoid risks, be careful with your money, and maintain a solid financial situation. Instead of relying on windfall earnings, attempt to acquire things gently and consistently.

Love: This card represents consistency and commitment in a partnership. This partnership will be based on practical considerations such as sexual delights and financial stability. In such situations, you must stay honest and patient with yourself and your partner.

Career: This is the time to advocate for self-sufficiency. To be successful, you must rely on your hard work and endurance. This card also suggests that a job can yield fruitful results. Farming, manufacturing or construction are examples of possible occupations.

Queen of Wands

Element: Fire

Astrological signs: Aries, Leo, Sagittarius

Upright: Pragmatic, affectionate, autonomous

Reversed: Extra onus, revengeful, maternal

Card description: The Queen of Wands features a monarch sitting erect on her throne carved with lions facing opposite directions, a symbol of fire and strength. She holds a sunflower, a symbol of joy, contentment and fertility in her left hand. She holds a wand in her right hand. The wand is beginning to bloom, a sign of new life. The Queen of Wands' best qualities include loyalty, provision and hospitality. A black cat, a traditional symbol of witchcraft and the occult rests at her feet, implying that she has a hidden side that she can tap into with her keen intuition.

Personal growth: The Queen represents the dominance of the physical world. The card urges you to gain control over your finances and possessions. Enjoy, care for, and accept your own body. Start meditating on the Queen if your dream should become a reality.

About a person: The Queen of Wands, as a person, represents those who are passionate and ambitious. They have a dazzling and amiable air and tend to be quite extroverted. Such individuals are fundamentally extremely sociable beings with a propensity to spread joy and happiness. They also have a strong feeling of their own worth and will not tolerate being disparaged by others. They strive for professional success and almost always succeed in doing so.

Money: You should bear in mind that financial gains are made through successful investments or business initiatives. To succeed, you must use your money and other resources constructively and creatively, focusing on collaborative financial endeavours. You must handle your money wisely.

Love: The Queen of Pentacles depicts a mature relationship between people who are truthful in their feelings. Respect, fulfilment, sensual pleasure, protection, and mutual support will be the foundations of any association.

Career: The Queen represents collaborative ventures, coordination, and alliance, indicating that you have a competitive advantage in business and a good understanding of people management. Supplement financial incentives with a job. In a health-related industry, your work will benefit others, and people will rely on you for financial support.

King of Wands

Element: Fire

Astrological signs: Aries, Leo, Sagittarius

Upright: Attractive, truce-maker, optimism

Reversed: Egoistic, confidential, unstable

Card description: The King of Wands features a man holding a blossoming wand, symbolising originality and drive. His throne and cape feature the salamander and the lion, symbols of fire and strength. The salamanders biting their own tails represent both infinity and the will to persevere in the face of overwhelming odds. The cape is fiery orange, like a flame. The crown is shaped like a tongue of fire. The King of Wands has a rich history of symbolism. It is time we dug into it.

Personal growth: You should be bold, decisive and inventive. Turn your principles into action. Approach life with zeal and assurance. Others will regard you with respect and loyalty if you treat them well.

About a person: The King of Wands, as a person, signifies that you are a born leader who exudes self-assurance and tenacity. The King of Wands will make a valiant effort to pursue their objectives and uphold their convictions. Although this inherent desire draws admiration, their outgoing and self-assured personalities attract people. The persuasiveness of those with a King of Wands personality assists others to be their best selves.

Money: Honesty and steadiness are necessary in financial dealings. This card indicates a large-scale project that offers success but may require effort and attention. It could also imply that financial assistance is available or that a spouse is reliable.

Love: This card denotes a loving relationship between two people. Both are devoted to one another. The importance of loyalty cannot be overstated. Expect someone who is already in a relationship to stay with their partner. The card also advises you to express your feelings without stopping them.

Career: This is the leader's card, and it advises you to take charge, show leadership abilities, and inspire trust in others when it emerges. Decisiveness and ambition are two qualities that you should possess. Now is an excellent time for others to notice your efforts and talents. You may get involved in a creative endeavour or a worthwhile cause.

Suit of Cups

Important things to note about Cups

Water is its element. The primary information they exhibit is how we uphold our sentiments. The cup has so much in it that you can field questions on many issues, be it a boon or bane.

You must enunciate with the Cups to come under their purview and get the answers connected with your personal life.

Upright position of these cards indicates innovation, satisfaction, kindness, feeling of ecstasy, enjoyable life, to relish.

Reversed position of these cards indicates abhorrence, strong sexual desire, lamentation.

Ace of Cups

Element: Water

Astrological signs: Cancer, Scorpio, Pisces

Upright: Satisfaction, loyal, innovative

Reversed: Infertility, low morale, loneliness

ACE OF CUPS

Card description: In the Ace of Cups, a hand from the clouds extends a cup to the querent. This cup overflows with pure and sparkling water, representing the purity of your feelings. If you accept this offer, drinking from this cup will unquestionably enrich your life on every level—physical, mental, and spiritual.

The brim of the cup is overflowing with water in five separate streams. The cup represents the subconscious mind and the streams, the five senses. This illustrates the emotions and the power of intuition. The vast ocean flows below the hand, signifying the awakening of the human spirit. The Ace of Cups suggests that the querent should listen to their intuition and always be honest with themselves, no matter what, to achieve the emotional or spiritual fulfilment represented by the card. This will require self-control of your emotions, but the message on the card suggests the payoff could be immense happiness.

Number association: You'll know when something new with a lot of potential is coming if your readings contain a lot of aces. They are merely formless pure energy, and it is up to you to mould the same and materialise the potential they stand for. They are unstable because they are raw. If you are not careful, they can overwhelm you very soon.

Personal growth: You must open your heart to love on the levels of person and spirituality or both. You can sense a feeling of connectedness. You can also reflect joyful feelings to others. To strengthen your creativity and intuition, focus on this card.

About a person: The Ace of Cups, as a person, is a loving person who is spiritually attuned. Their instincts, creativity, and intuition help them make moral decisions throughout their lives. People with an Ace of Cups personality are intuitive and wise beyond their years. Once someone finds their 'home', they never leave. They say that 'home is where the heart is'. Their capacity for unconditional love is influenced by this quality. This person strikes me as being unique and unusual. Their eyes frequently have a sparkle to them. Many are healers and psychics.

Money: You can launch creative and profit-giving initiatives. If you can nurture your inspiration, you can produce excellent financial results. In matters that involve money, you must pay attention to your intuition.

Love: The card signals the beginning of a new relationship. It describes the initial stages of romance, where two people identify their mutual attraction. If you want to blossom, then nurture this growing relationship.

Career: You will definitely feel passionate about your job and the project you are beginning. You can actualise a long-realised dream. This activity may also spark your creativity. If you want to maximise this opportunity, invest your time and effort.

Two of Cups

Element: Water

Astrological signs: Cancer, Scorpio, Pisces

Upright: Comprehending, new relations, love

Reversed: Ditch, break up, disjointed

Card description: The Two of Cups shows a man and a woman ceremonially exchanging cups. The Caduceus of Hermes (a winged staff with two snakes wrapped around it) floats above them in the middle, a symbol associated with compromise, commerce, the cosmos, security, etiquette and duality. The Two of Cups is one of the most positive cards in the tarot deck, and it portends well for any kind of relationship: romantic, professional, or otherwise. A new partnership is on the horizon and will be forged with equilibrium, respect, and honour. The chimera, which represents fire and passion, sits atop the Caduceus and governs not only this partnership but also the relationship itself.

Number association: The topic of the twos is pairing up, with all the complications that this union entails. We go from the oneness, and the twos offer a glimpse of togetherness. The twos typically stand for harmony and the coming together of opposing elements to form a whole. This harmony can occasionally be so flawless that it makes it impossible to move on and causes paralysis when a decision needs to be taken.

Personal growth: Learn the art of give-and-take. The card also symbolises the different facets of one's own personality that can unite. If you want to encourage harmony and cooperation, meditate on this card.

About a person: The Two of Cups, as a person, is a warm, loving and lovely individual. They are passionate about establishing and keeping enduring relationships. This usually suggests that the individual will get married young and continue to be in a committed relationship. They make excellent friends, children, siblings and lovers because they emphasise on fostering relationships. Due to their propensity for listening to their partners and responding with wise counsel, they are frequently natural healers.

Money: The card indicates combined resources and partnerships related to business. You will benefit greatly from the capital of the network and your partner's abilities. However, the reverse is also equally possible. Unite efforts can improve the prospects of earning profit for both of you.

Love: The two indicates the flow of affection between two people in a harmonious manner. You will nourish each other because of your emotional reciprocity and intuitive understanding. You will enjoy a happy, balanced relationship based on mutual respect, equality and caring and bring out the best in each other.

Career: The card indicates a partnership based on creativity where two people combine their skills and create the desired output. Combined abilities can give you better results compared to individual abilities. Look forward to creating equity and cooperation in your workplace.

Three of Cups

Element: Water

Astrological signs: Cancer, Scorpio, Pisces

Upright: Fertile, imagination, happiness

Reversed: Lecherous, self-centred, destruction

Card description: The Three of Cups shows three women dancing in a circle, holding their cups aloft. Their floral crowns indicate their high spirits and the wreaths they are waving a sign of their hard-won triumph. They are on a field of flowers and fruit, further emphasising the optimistic message of the card. The women all feel a sense of awe, respect, compassion and happiness.

Number association: The tarot's threes are governed by group dynamics, and they represent many events that might happen when groups of people or ideas join. It also denotes an initial completion of a first phase of some kind because it is also conceptualised symbolically as completion (the first polygon, the Holy Trinity, etc).

Personal growth: This is the time to understand that you should embrace what others have to serve you and contribute what you have. This is the moment to promote spiritual friendliness while resolving disagreements with others

About a person: The Three of Cups, as a person, is empathetic and cheerful. Since they enjoy being the centre of attention, they have many friends with whom they enjoy spending time. This person's charisma, beauty, and sense of style will make an impression wherever they go. You can never be unhappy with a Three of Cups person because they are always eager to make new friends and spread happiness. Others around them can be jealous of this person's flamboyant lifestyle. They always seem to land on their feet and find a way to make new friends wherever they go.

Money: An investment made with others can help you receive benefits and rewards. Good outcomes may result due to collective financial effort. You should use your resources for the good of your household, society and humankind.

Love: This is the ideal time to spread happiness and love to others. The card depicts a pleasant emotion that goes beyond a longing for a romantic connection. It also denotes a strong tie with family, friendships, and people you care about. The card indicates weddings or romantic ceremonies.

Career: Positive outcomes are likely to be obtained in an employment situation. As a result of the joint efforts of a group, you will encounter good fortune. The card also informs your participation in a creative joint venture or celebrating your victory with others.

Four of Cups

Element: Water

Astrological signs: Cancer, Scorpio, Pisces

Upright: Tired, tensed, proud

Reversed: Gratitude, focus, enthusiasm

Card description: The Four of Cups depicts a young man, alone and sitting under a tree on a mountaintop. He has his legs and hands crossed. He is in meditation or deep contemplation. Three empty cups sit in front of him on the grass, and an outstretched arm offers him the fourth. He does not seem to be notice this or interested as he is engrossed in his thoughts.

The Four of Cups is a symbol of our propensity to take the things we have for granted, which makes it difficult for us to recognise the gifts the universe is trying to give us at any given moment. The solutions to our problems are usually within reach, but we are too preoccupied with what we lack to notice them.

Number association: The number four typically denotes the establishment of a foundation. The goal here is to grow and evolve since, even if the foundation has been laid, there may occasionally be some disappointment because things may not have gone as planned. The fours are, therefore, another way the universe encourages us to advance and flourish.

Personal growth: The card represents boredom and stagnation. This is the moment to reflect and figure out what you desire. Also, investigate your soul for the decisions you have taken that have led you to a point of dissatisfaction.

About a person: The Four of Cups, as a person, is unhappy with how their life is now unfolding. This individual lacks the motivation to pursue happiness, which causes them to turn down opportunities that might otherwise fulfil their wishes and desires. As a result, this person's life is unhappy. This card shows resistance. The individual depicted on the card does not want the golden cup offered to them by the mystical hand that appears on the card.

Money: You can feel trapped by your own things or use money to satisfy your emotional demands if you are emotionally attached to money. You might be attempting to let your emotions control your financial decisions. There are signs of financial stability, but this is not a growth issue.

Love: Because of the emphasis on stability and routine, excitement and progress may be lacking in a relationship, or your happiness may be jeopardised. As a result, you may experience boredom or irritation with your partner, or the relationship or you may come to an end. Now is the moment to assess your priorities and choose what you truly desire in life.

Career: Your job may make you feel trapped or restricted. However, you are prioritising security and comfort over all else, which is why you should always reevaluate your priorities. Our existing work environment no longer challenges or fulfils you. Now is the time to hunt for another job that will provide you with better opportunities and progress.

Five of Cups

Element: Water

Astrological signs: Cancer, Scorpio, Pisces

Upright: Fear, wasteful efforts, comatose, misfortune

Reversed: Recovering, forgiving, acceptance

Card description: The Five of Cups is one of the tarot cards that carries a lot of weight because of the negative feelings it can evoke. This card represents not only the loss itself but also the difficulties that arise as a result of that loss.

A person in a black cloak appears on the card. The person covers his face, seemingly out of sadness. Two of the five cups are still upright, and the others lie on the floor. However, the individual doesn't seem to realise that there are two standing cups because he is too preoccupied with his grief. Though the two cups represent new opportunities, the man is upset with his losses. In the distance, he sees a home or castle, but a raging river separates him from it, representing the flood of feelings that have driven him away.

Number association: The fives stand for transition, change, turbulence, and strife (at times). The fives come after the fours and amplify the same energy. The fives encourage us to seek within for a deeper cause for why to move forward when that energy explodes. We must advance to overcome this instability and go forward.

Personal growth: The card denotes a need for change and open dependence. You have already outgrown your current circumstance. Therefore, you need to move on, even if that means emotionally letting go of people or things.

About a person: The Five of Cups, as a person, may not be easy to win over. These folks frequently view things negatively and are gloomy. Some people struggle to start afresh due to their focus on the past. They are also highly emotional people who would rather play the blame game than try to acknowledge and learn from their mistakes. They don't love themselves and frequently put their health and well-being last. Despite all of this, they may be loyal, understanding friends to individuals going through difficult circumstances. Nevertheless, as soon as they attempt to move on and embrace optimism, the Five of Cups will turn against their pals and accuse them of being conceited.

Money: The card depicts loss and disappointment, but only for some time. You have not gotten the expected results from an investment, or you have incurred unforeseen costs. Don't give up hope or give good money to dishonest people. While cutting your losses, go on to something greater.

Love: If your relationship has not lived up to your expectations and blossomed, you may be upset, but now isn't the time to wallow in self-pity or anger; instead, take the necessary steps to douse the fire. As a result of the temporary separation, you may be able to see things more clearly. The five represents the conclusion of a miserable relationship and the beginning of a significantly better and more satisfying one.

Career: You may be completely dissatisfied with your effort. You may also have the impression, that neither your worth nor your abilities are fully utilised. It is possible that a situation will not turn out the way you imagined. It is time to let go of the past and move on to something more gratifying and appreciative.

Six of Cups

Element: Water

Astrological signs: Cancer, Scorpio, Pisces

Upright: Concord, ripe good dividends, cheerful time

Reversed: Fear of confrontation, yearning, monotony

Card description: The Six of Cups represents homey warmth, childhood innocence, and the pleasure of remembering happier times. The card features six cups brimming with white flowers. A young boy in the foreground is handing a young girl one of the cups. This symbolises the continuity of rituals and the joy of reconnecting with old friends. The children are in the garden of a large house, representing a sense of safety and contentment.

Number association*:* The sixes, in contrast to the fives, which indicate conflict, symbolise the transition from that conflict into a resolution, whether internal or external, whether it indicates reconciliation or letting go. They represent the triumph over adversity and the dawning of light.

Personal growth: Six represents the return of happier times and emotional regeneration. Your generosity, inventiveness and clarity will shine through in all your undertakings. Share what you have with others openly and gladly. You can be confident that your presents will be appreciated. You will have more happiness and harmony in your life.

About a person: The Six of Cups, as a person, brings harmony and balance to any group. You can always rely on them when you are in a bind or need sound guidance. Their constant benevolence outweighs their often-infantile naivety, which makes them naive to the world around them. Along with having a good sense of style, Six of Cups personalities frequently decorate their homes and choose fashionable attire.

Money: A link between the past and the present in terms of money, it's represented by this card. This is a card of renewal and denotes a debt repayment or a return to a more financially secure position following a long time of insecurity and instability. The card also represents a give-and-take in financial matters, such as sharing profits and expenses.

Love: In a partnership, joy and affection are freely exchanged. Now that you are ready to show your love for your partner and your feelings have been reciprocated, your love will strengthen because the impediments have vanished. In other situations, the return of an old lover or the reawakening of romance after a period of stalemate may happen.

Career: You may see a resurgence of excitement for your work. Either your perception or circumstances have changed, allowing you to be more innovative and successful. You have learnt new abilities that will help you advance in your career. You will be devoted to your previous efforts. I appreciated being involved in the workplace, and it will continue to improve.

Seven of Cups

Element: Water

Astrological signs: Cancer, Scorpio, Pisces

Upright: Inventive, will to succeed, options

Reversed: Hallucinations, feeling trapped, lack of choice

Card description: The Seven of Cups symbolises fantasy, wishful thinking, illusion, imagination and choice. The image on the card depicts a person with their back turned to us, looking at seven cups filled with gifts. These cups are all floating in the clouds. Clouds symbolise imaginings, fantasies, and other mental constructs such as dreams and illusions. Some cups hold gifts such as jewels and wreaths, whereas others hold dangers like snakes and dragons. The many phantasms erupting from the cups are a metaphor for the myriad images that run through one's head while dreaming. If you draw the Seven of Cups, it could mean you have many choices available.

Number association: When there are several sevens in a reading, it typically means it is time to take a step back and reflect. The sevens challenge us to rethink and assess whether the course we are on, is the best one for us. Although it can occasionally feel lonely, this phase is necessary if you want to go forward with your true desires.

Personal growth: The card symbolises a period of great inspiration and emotional exploration if you use your imagination to create the settings in your life. Fear should not hold you back; instead, keep your mind open to new possibilities.

About a person: The Seven of Cups, as a person, is disengaged from reality and prone to getting caught up in lofty ideals. They have inflated expectations for themselves and are ill-equipped to deal with the unpleasant effects of their own failings. Because they are unable to adequately protect themselves, they need to be cautious around abusive persons. They may experience bullying.

Money: Money is shaped by fantasy and idealistic thinking. Even after much brainstorming, you may be coming up with many money-making strategies. But you may also think that none of them will succeed. You tend to be overly optimistic. Some offers or programmes may be deceptive, so investigate them thoroughly. Use your imagination to come up with new ways to make money.

Love: On the one hand, you are trying to figure out what kind of relationship you want, and on the other, you have romantic fancies. You cannot have it all, so choose what is most important. The card depicts an emotionally inspired interaction between you and another person that encourages creativity and imagination.

Career: Try exploring different career opportunities and possibilities. You may not be realistic about your employment or future. The card indicates a job that can boost your creativity to find what is best for you, try exploring different career opportunities and possibilities. It is possible that you are not realistic. An opportunity that appears to be too good to be true, on the other hand, should be carefully explored.

Eight of Cups

Element: Water

Astrological signs: Cancer, Scorpio, Pisces

Upright: Versatile, growth, away from enemies

Reversed: Illusionary world, queasiness, efforts not fruitful

Card description: The Eight of Cups forces us to face the transition period. A masked individual leaves behind eight golden cups before departing for an uninhabited region. He has grown disenchanted with his cup collection and is now leaving them behind in search of more meaningful pursuits. This could indicate the result of the disappointment in a person in finding that the thing they have been striving for in life is not as exciting or fulfilling as they had hoped.

It could also symbolise someone seeking adventure in the form of a challenge. The desolate, mountainous regions they travel to, represent, in a broader sense, the prospect of undertaking new challenges. It is as if their stark emptiness is inviting someone to come along and give them form. Exploring new territory can take the form of engaging in activities with the potential to foster personal development on multiple levels.

It is a sign of the resolve to focus on one's own development, learning, and improvement rather than on the success or failure of others.

Number association: The eights signify the end of a second phase and typically represent some form of accomplishment, whether it be materialistic or emotional. Here, growth may occur in both directions, and it occasionally manifests itself in ways, we least expect.

Personal growth: You should be more sincere as you seek your life's mission and cease concentrating on all those things that give significance to your existence and all those people and activities that divert you from your path.

About a person: The Eight of Cups is a person with a marked desire to leave the material world in search of prosperity and true happiness. This person has recently accepted who they really are and realised that those around them don't share their priorities. The card indicates a breakup, a change in career, or even a profound spiritual trip. The Eight of Cups represents introverted individuals who are more interested in spiritual topics and deeper meanings of things than they are in making new acquaintances. As a result, getting to know these folks can be difficult. They are frequently highly guarded people who require some time before feeling secure enough to be transparent.

Money: Now is the moment to focus on utilising your assets. If you want to grow and thrive, you must fully commit your heart, mind, and energy. Hold on to our investments indefinitely and only give them to people who truly deserve them or abandon something if it is not profitable in some situations.

Love: A committed relationship will have a great impact on you; now is the time to be genuine and commit to your spouse. Rather than casual interactions, you anticipate a deep and meaningful commitment. The card may also suggest a poor relationship that cannot be saved.

Career: You may put your whole heart and soul into your work. Pay close attention to the details. Allow nothing to deter you from achieving your goal. You can attain your wildest aspirations, if you are determined to work for what you truly want. This card suggests that you may leave a career you have outgrown.

Nine of Cups

Element: Water

Astrological signs: Cancer, Scorpio, Pisces

Upright: Strong senses, festive, genial

Reversed: Excessive pride, satisfied, pin-pointing others

Card description: This card shows a middle-aged man seated on a wooden bench, his arms crossed and a smile on his face. He appears to be quite content with his life. He exudes an air of refined sophistication and appears to be in complete contentment with his life. The red headdress on his head symbolises the fiery nature of his mind. You can see nine golden cups arranged uniformly in an arch on the background. The Nine of Cups is a tarot card that represents attaining one's goals and being successful in both a spiritual and material sense. Following the fulfilment of his deepest aspiration, the man displays a look of contentment on his face.

Number association: The nines suggest close to completion, which could mean reaching a plateau. What appears to be the finish line might be a temporary stage. Even though there is a sense of finality, this is typically just a brief period before the cycle's conclusion.

Personal growth: The number nine denotes ease and satisfaction, indicating that you should not try or fight. You have earned great fulfilment and peace of mind, and the time to enjoy it has arrived. So chill and enjoy it. By sitting quietly on this card, you can strengthen your luck.

About a person: The Nine of Cups, as a person, loves life and lives it to the fullest. This person has a positive self-image. It is difficult to determine if the Nine of Cups attains success because of their confidence or the other way around. But either way, they always obtain what they want. They place a lot of importance on appearances and frequently live extravagant lives in every manner. They are genuinely content and at ease in their own skin; this is not just some façade they put on for the sake of others. They thus possess a carefree, loving, and optimistic view of life.

Money: The card denotes prosperity and good fortune. This card is also known as the wish card. It forecasts financial or business success since you have applied your true self. You will acquire money, which will bring you happiness.

Love: You are on your way to a great and rewarding life and will enjoy it. Whether you are looking for a helpful and loyal spouse, your fantasies are coming true. Knowing what you genuinely want and pursuing it is the best approach to happiness.

Career: Fortunately, you were successful in your career, and now is the time to locate the right job or advance in your chosen profession. Now is the moment to reap the benefits of what you have accomplished. Wishes would come true when this card occurs. This is because you are fine-tuning yourself and the time you invest.

Ten of Cups

Element: Water

Astrological signs: Cancer, Scorpio, Pisces

Upright: Promise, tranquil, feeling of happiness

Reversed: Destructive mind, lazy, separation

Card description: The tarot card known as the Ten of Cups depicts a scene of a couple holding each other while looking towards a lovely house and a lush garden. Two young children are having a wonderful time playing next to them. While the couple are in an affectionate and romantic embrace, the children are seen running around and having fun. The couple appears to have a healthy relationship, in addition to being blessed with a pleasant home and lovely children. The tranquil flow of the river signifies the unimpeded expression of emotions between the couple, suggesting that their relationship is harmonious. The green land indicates fertility and shows that the land is fertile. The ten cups in the sky are arranged in an arch and represent blessings from above. The rainbow in the background represents the end of difficult times and sorrows, as well as the beginning of a new happy life that the entire family can take pleasure in. The Ten of Cups is a card that symbolises success and fulfilment in life.

Number association: In the tens, we see the actual end of the cycle, that something has come full circle; this denotes that moving forward, we can head towards a fresh start.

Personal growth: The card denotes fulfilment and personal achievement. Because you are now content with your present life and are compatible with yourself, you are able to relate to others in a sensible and genuine manner.

About a person: The Ten of Cups, as a person, is spiritual and kind. But they can sometimes become so focused on perfection that it causes problems for those around them. Those symbolised by the Ten of Cups are typically successful since they are diligent, likeable and hard-working. Additionally, they work hard to maintain it, which by nature puts their internal tranquilly in danger. They make a special effort to avoid unfavourable characters and circumstances, especially those that involve conflict. This thinking may result in such people leading somewhat sheltered, self-imposed lives. Unfortunately, this poses a threat to their inner peace since, rather than engaging in a dispute, they might sacrifice their own positions and best interests due to their strong desire to avoid conflict. Finally, this causes resentment and hatred directed internally, which is obviously antithetical to the internal harmony that so clearly distinguishes them.

Money: The card denotes a period of prosperity and awards. At this point, your efforts will pay off and you will get dividends from financial ventures. It is possible to achieve immediate opposition to initial security and ease. This card has been used to represent family or inherited wealth from the family business.

Love: The card depicts fulfilment, maturity, a helpful and caring partnership, and a happy lifestyle. You will feel comfortable and secure if you belong to a family or a group of like-minded people.

Career: It is time to be appreciated and acknowledged for your efforts. You will gain respect, awards, and happiness for the work and abilities you've demonstrated. The card can also reflect a family's united activity or employment.

Page of Cups

Element: Water

Astrological signs: Cancer, Scorpio, Pisces

Upright: Imaginative, liking, regarding

Reversed: Possessive, planning and plotting, self-interested

Card description: The Page of Cups symbolises the mysterious insights that can strike at any time. The card shows a young man holding a golden cup and standing on the beach. He wears a blue tunic with floral prints. A long, flowing scarf trails from a bohemian-looking beret. Like something out of a fairy tale, a fish swims out of the cup and surprises him. The unexpected appearance of the fish indicates that inspiration can come out of the blue.

Possible events: Be careful of your fickle-minded attitude towards love, and pay special attention to what your near and dear ones are suggesting to you. Spare no stone unturned to get desired results.

Personal growth: This is the time to strengthen your self-confidence. The card can also signify a strong intuition or a genuine creative talent that can assist you to the next level.

About a person: The Page of Cups, as a person, possesses a robust sense of intuition and is intensely aware of all the dimensions present in his immediate environment. They have a kind and pleasing personality, and they have a strong desire to be with people who share their beliefs since doing so makes them feel valued and gives them a sense of being special. They are highly imaginative and sentimental. They tend to be reserved and anxious to avoid conflict, but they won't back down from a fight if necessary.

Money: In questions about money, you may be untrained. You are a trustworthy individual, but you are incompetent at handling funds and resources. The card also represents financial insecurity and warns that a commercial transaction is not well-established or grounded.

Love: Because of past bad experiences, you feel insecure and hesitant regarding relationships. As a result, you may become overly self-absorbed or go to the opposite extreme and refuse to allow anyone to approach you. Before you can begin to experience a joyful connection, you must first let go of your previous sorrow and restore your self-esteem.

Career: Either you may be deeply attached to your profession, or you can connect your self-worth with it. However, you are both naïve and foolish when trusting others. Take a stand for yourself, and do not let others govern you. Don't put yourself in a difficult situation.

Knight of Cups

Element: Water

Astrological signs: Cancer, Scorpio, Pisces

Upright: Passionate, imaginative, excited

Reversed: Inhumane, bilk, insincere

Card description: This card, known as the Knight of Cups, depicts a young man riding a white horse and holding a cup, suggesting he is a messenger. When contrasted with the Knight of Wands and the Knight of Swords, this person is not riding aggressively forward on his horse. Instead, he moves slowly forward, creating a sense of calm and serenity in the environment. Many cultures see the horse as a symbol of vitality, strength and power. The colour white, like that of the horse, is commonly associated with enlightenment, innocence and purity.

Possible events: Shape your feeling before getting into any relationship, emotional blackmailing.

Personal growth: You should take a chance and face difficulties. Take advantage of fresh opportunities. Instead of hesitating, stick to things and see them through. If you have a commitment, keep it.

About a person: The Knight of Cups, as a person, represents an individual who is artistic and sensitive and is constantly engaged in some form of creative effort, whether it is creating a song, a screenplay, a novel, or just making notes on their phone. Knight of Cups people are immensely charming and likeable when they want to or need to be. They may be amorous. You may encounter someone like them when travelling, and it goes without saying that they make their living through the arts. Those born under the sign of the Knight of Cups are highly sexual beings.

Money: If your finances are stagnating, a movement can bring you good fortune. New initiatives may be helpful. The card also suggests that your indecisiveness, hesitancy, and lack of loyalty stop you from reaping the benefits you deserve. The card also warns of new-born circumstances, so the opportunity is not what it appears to be.

Love: Uncertainty or apprehension about commitment can prevent you from having a great relationship. You want to be able to choose from a variety of possibilities continuously. You also fear that allowing the other person to get too close to you may cause them to hurt or dominate you. The Knight signifies a cheerful sensation in a romance free of expectations and a highly charged relationship with an imaginative person on a few occasions.

Career: If you feel blocked, you will need to change jobs. Because you are unable to commit to a job, inconsistency inhibits you from growing. For all creative people, the Knight provides a chance to put one's talents and ideas to good use.

Queen of Cups

Element: Water

Astrological signs: Cancer, Scorpio, Pisces

Upright: Creative, love, predictable

Reversed: Waste, lack of love, not honest

QUEEN of CUPS.

Card description: The Queen of Cups is in charge of our feelings. Her throne sits on the ocean shore; the ocean, a body of water often used as a metaphor for the subconscious and emotions. Sitting on the throne, she represents the space between land and sea, the realm of emotion and reason. She holds a cup with handles shaped like angels. The closed cup suggests that her feelings come from the unconscious mind. The Queen enjoys her time alone in contemplation. The tranquillity of the sea and sky indicates the peaceful disposition of the Queen. She can observe her innermost emotions and thoughts without getting overwhelmed ,because her feet are above the water.

Possible events: Sometimes behave as if your senses are not in your control, the time to learn love is not known by words but by deeds.

Personal growth: Whether you are a woman or a man, it's time to embrace your feminine side. By meditating on the card, you can enhance your imagination and intuition while also strengthening your compassion and acceptance.

About a person: The Queen of Cups, as a person, is a mature person who is kind, loving and supportive; who is always there for you when you need them. Because of their innate generosity, inherent empathy, and genuine concern for the lives and well-being of others, Queen of Cups people frequently have an attentive disposition. Some tend to be a bit more reserved than is healthy for them, while others have a far greater sense of insecurity about their significant creative abilities—something that is common to many artists but is exaggerated to the extreme in this case. They tend to be joyful, charismatic individuals who enjoy appreciating art almost as much as they like creating it.

Money: You can utilise your intuition and financial knowledge, but do not forget to employ basic logic and pragmatism. If the situation is perplexing, you must be flexible at that time. Your artistic sense can help you considerably.

Love: This is not the time to judge others or expect them to satisfy your wishes, as the Queen plainly depicts nurturing unconditional love and acceptance. Be flexible when it comes to matters of the heart. The card also suggests that you will be picky about who you choose as your spouse. Allow them to be self-sufficient, but not at your expense.

Career: Use your ideas and ingenuity to create high-quality, inspiring work. There is a greater probability that your professional path or workplace will change. Be flexible at work. The card also denotes a job more geared toward women.

King of Cups

Element: Water

Astrological signs: Cancer, Scorpio, Pisces

Upright: Unbiased, bold, conventional

Reversed: Short-tempered, partial, despotic

Card description: According to the tarot, the King of Cups represents openness, mastery and equilibrium in one's feelings. The image on the card is of a king sitting atop a throne, wearing a fish-shaped amulet. The fish pendant on his necklace is a metaphor for his free spirit and inventive mind, which flourish in the tranquil waters of his life. Consciousness and unconsciousness appear to maintain a stable equilibrium in the background.

The king wears a blue tunic and a gold cape, showing his status. He holds a cup in his right hand and a sceptre in his left. To the right of the king is a fish that appears to be leaping out of the water, representing the realm of emotion. To the left of the king, a ship, representing the realm of matter, is present. The king appears balanced and in control of his emotions. The King of Cups indicates that you should not try to control or stifle your emotions. Instead, you have developed the skills necessary to respond to them healthily.

Possible events: Think wisely, your set principle makes you more potent than ever before.

Personal growth: Develop the ability to trust and be trusted by others. It is unnecessary to put yourself in a vulnerable situation by disclosing yourself. By meditating on this card, you will become more open and accepting.

About a person: The King of Cups is a perfect mix of positive male and female energy. As a result, they have pure hearts and are kind, loving and generous. They exude a gentle authority that commands respect, which their friends, co-workers, and even casual acquaintances immediately accord to them. They are also worldly with excellent emotional intelligence. Although they sometimes seem aloof and uninterested in other people's problems, you can be sure that they still pay attention. They are usually kind and want what is best for you. They engage in politics occasionally and are naturally polite but rarely, if ever, run for office. King of Cups folks are experts in the emotional world in many ways.

Money: Your feelings may be influencing your financial or commercial decisions. It is time to take charge of all issues involving financial resources and investments while being thoughtful of others. If you dedicate yourself entirely to adventure, your chances of success increase.

Love: All that is necessary is trust, commitment and loyalty. You want to be in a relationship, but you or your partner are frightened of losing control if you express your emotions. In romantic relationships, the card also represents secrecy and defensiveness. It can represent emotional maturity and the ability to protect, nurture and empathise with a spouse.

Career: The King demonstrates a friend's wish, which can lead to power disputes. As a result of a concern of losing ground to someone else, someone you work with may become too protective. The card suggests that you should help others. Make use of your imagination and intuition.

Suit of Swords

It is the third suit of Minor Arcana.

Swords are associate with wisdom, thoughtfulness, courage, and a constructive approach.

Cards in upright position indicate being unbiased, discipline, good management and accuracy.

Cards in reversed position indicate mischievousness, feeling of ill will, vulnerable to diseases, and difference of opinion.

Ace of Swords

Element: Air

Astrological signs: Gemini, Libra, Aquarius

Upright: Triumph, wise, flexible

Reversed: Bias, anarchical behaviour, demolition

ACE of SWORDS.

Card description: A hand appears from a white cloud in the Ace of Swords, brandishing a two-sided blade. This two-edged sword is crowned in gold and encircled by a wreath. Traditionally, the wreath has represented triumph and honour for a long time.

The crown is the universally recognised symbol of royalty as well as the authority to rule that comes along with being royal.

The sword floats in front of a dynamic background that includes mountains and the sea as metaphors for the vast territory and faraway lands that can be conquered with these weapons and for the desire to achieve greatness.

Number association: You'll know when something new with a lot of potential is coming if your readings contain a lot of aces. They are merely formless pure energy, and it is up to you to mould them and materialise the potential they stand for. They are unstable because they are raw, and if you don't take care, they can overwhelm you very soon.

Personal growth: The Ace of Swords represents concentration and attention. It does, however, require you to be fairer and more reasonable. It also serves as a signal for a significant new thought or point of view.

About a person: The Ace of Swords, as a person, is exceedingly intelligent, full of brilliant ideas, and successful at using the power of thought. They are not excessively emotional. They prefer using reason and reasoning to solve their difficulties rather than listening to their hearts. Also, they are fierce competitors who frequently outwit and outperform their rivals. They take chances and aim to excel in any pastime, profession, or interest they want to pursue. This is caused in part by their inability to sit still for extended periods and their propensity to lose themselves in their thoughts when given an excessive amount of alone time.

Money: A new idea can get off the ground and lead to profit. The card might also represent a communication-related endeavour. You should trust yourself and emphasise your purpose. A primary-level negotiation about a deal involving funds may happen.

Love: The Ace of Swords also denotes the attributes of a mate who is emotionally unattached but mentally oriented. The card indicates that a relationship will begin shortly based on shared views and friendship. You should take part in a dialogue or discussion about relationship concerns in a direct manner.

Career: There may be a starting point for a project or vocation that will require you to use your brain, communication skills, and public sources. Do not let anyone distract you or focus from concentrating on your goal. In some circumstances, you should upskill yourself to improve your career prospects.

Two of Swords

Element: Air

Astrological signs: Gemini, Libra, Aquarius

Upright: Balanced state, calm, supporters

Reversed: Strain, disguise, unkind

Card description: When presented with challenging options, the Two of Swords represents the muddled thinking that often results. The Two of Swords depicts a seated woman who is blindfolded and holding two swords. The sea is in the background, and the crags and rocks represent obstacles. The woman on the card is blindfolded to symbolise a situation that prevents her from seeing the problem or the solution.

The fact that she is wielding a sword in each hand illustrates that two paths are present but oppose one another and do not share any common ground. It is also possible that it represents a standstill which indicates that the issue at hand needs to be solved using logical reasoning. The moon on the right-hand side of the card shows that illusions and deceptions play a significant part in the challenges that the woman faces when trying to make a decision.

Number association: The topic of the twos is pairing up, with all the complications that this union entails. We go from the oneness, and the twos offer a glimpse of togetherness. The twos typically stand for harmony and the coming together of opposing elements to form a whole. This harmony can occasionally be so flawless that it makes it impossible to move on and causes paralysis when you have to decide.

Personal growth: Since the future is unknown, you must rely on faith alone. The card also suggests you improve your focus, become more reasonable, and learn more about a topic. In whatever you do, try to find serenity and harmony.

About a person: The Two of Swords, as a person, seeks balance in all facets of life. They detest conflict and poisonous settings more than anything because they think maintaining equilibrium is essential to leading a peaceful life. They frequently make significant concessions to avoid upsetting people, demonstrating that their judgements are heavily influenced by how they will be perceived by others. Those symbolised by the Two of Swords have a strong desire to care for others but struggle to be open and honest with those closest to them. In a new relationship, you shouldn't count on this person to open up at once because they probably have a very private nature.

Money: In the case of an engagement or a money-making enterprise, there may be a difference of opinion. There will be periods of uncertainty, but do not allow others to deceive you. Start trusting your own thoughts. Start strengthening your fundamentals. Notice whether any financial records, investments or agreements have any loopholes.

Love: A situation that appears tranquil on the surface may be fraught with conflict beneath the surface. Some of the difficulties must be identified and solved. In an attempt to overcome relationship issues, next-level communication and the power of tolerance are valued and advised.

Career: Lack of clarity can lead to misunderstanding in a work-related assignment. Even if you have a doubt about the conclusion, have faith in yourself and take care of any new details. Occasionally the meaning of two swords is a deadlock due to a disagreement of opinion. In order to deal with a difficult scenario, tactful abilities may be required. Do not try to pt things off.

Three of Swords

Element: Air

Astrological signs: Gemini, Libra, Aquarius

Upright: Unhappiness, loss, confusion

Reversed: Forgiving, compromise, healing

Card description: The Three of Swords features a floating heart pierced by three swords and is one of the most recognisable images in tarot cards. There are thick clouds in the sky above it. Rain is also falling heavily in the background. The impact on people's emotions is clear. The three swords represent the ability to harm, cause pain, and create suffering to what it pierces, while the heart represents love, affection and spirit. They portray the pain of loss and the ache of a broken heart. The clouds and rain reflect the overall gloomy atmosphere. The Three of Swords represents a low point in one's life, as suggested by these symbols. It also offers hope that the pain will soon disappear like the storm clouds.

Number association: The tarot's threes are governed by group dynamics, and they represent many events that might happen when groups of people or ideas join. It also denotes an initial completion of a first phase because it is also conceptualised symbolically as completion (the first polygon, the Holy Trinity, etc.).

Personal growth: The three words clearly indicate a heart-to-head misalignment. The dominant state of thought produces feelings of estrangement and gloominess. To solve this, you should take steps to connect with anything that feeds your spirit.

About a person: The Three of Swords, as a person, is clingy in their relationships to the point of shunning individuals because history has taught them to be envious, founded in their fear of being abandoned. They also have envy for others who they perceive to be free spirits. People with the Three of Swords are frequently challenging to love because they cannot be authentic and transparent. Some people struggle to settle down and become entire since they can only find fulfilment in another person. Their current personalities are overwhelmed by their past traumas.

Money: You may lose or suffer if you reject your intuition and rely solely on research and critical reasoning. This card can also indicate money obtained at the expense of other values or in a way that has caused suffering to others.

Love: There's a strong chance that you and the person you love have some differences. You may find yourself in a state of anguish and pain. Situations may occur that lead to arguments, stress, and physical separation. To avoid all of this, try to fill your life with kindness and understanding.

Career: You are not performing the work that you truly enjoy, and as a result, you are lonely, dissatisfied and regretful. This unhappiness, however, brings awareness, and once you know what you want to do, you can look for a better job. The time now is perfect for creative folks to use their time alone to develop and produce art that inspires others.

Four of Swords

Element: Air

Astrological signs: Gemini, Libra, Aquarius

Upright: Rejuvenate, give up

Reversed: Loneliness, crisis, deport

Card description: The Four of Swords represents an atmosphere of calm peace in stark contrast to the turmoil depicted by its counterpart, the Three of Swords. Upon this tomb in this church is carved the likeness of a knight, three swords hanging above him and the fourth lying at his feet. The three swords represents the pain he has been through. It appears the fight is over because the fourth sword is now in its sheathed position. The stained-glass of a child and a woman can be seen behind the statue, lending the scene an air of homeliness and welcome after the retreat. The knight's hands are folded before him like he is engrossed in prayer.

Number association: The number four typically denotes the establishment of a foundation. The goal here is to grow and evolve. Even if the foundation has been laid, there may occasionally be some disappointment because things may not have gone exactly as planned. The fours are, therefore, another way that the universe encourages us to advance and flourish.

Personal growth: The card represents isolation and reflection. Despite the hardships of the outside world, this is the best time to know yourself through meditation. Meditation, rest and spirituality are all recommended.

About a person: The Four of Swords, as a person, is a quiet, non-aggressive individual. They have gained the ability to get along

not succeed, others will. They are also self-delusional dreamers who find it difficult to admit their shortcomings as a result of their narcissistic and self-aggrandising mentality.

Money: It can be a source of indecision and confusion if you have financial troubles. This card can also reflect financial disagreements or conflicts of opinion. The influence of others may be causing you to be unable to see things clearly. Now is the time to shape yourself. This card can indicate that you are out of your league. Accepting restrictions or disappointments with decency is a good thing to do.

Love: You may be attempting to adjust as rapidly as possible. Confusion and unrest will occur as a result of this. It's good to listen to your mind and heart, but it's also a good idea to be open to new ideas and attempt to understand things from the other person's point of view. Instead of trying to get your way, seek understanding.

Career: Before you evolve, you need to first listen and understand. You may become puzzled and consequently hesitate to act or decide on issues. Indecisiveness has led to missed opportunities and failures; now is the moment to understand your limitations. Work for clarity and stay away from the problems of others. It is not a good time to make enemies.

not succeed, others will. They are also self-delusional dreamers who find it difficult to admit their shortcomings as a result of their narcissistic and self-aggrandising mentality,

Money: It can be a source of indecision and confusion if you have financial troubles. This card can also reflect financial disagreements or conflicts of opinion. The influence of others may be causing you to be unable to see things clearly. Now is the time to shape yourself. This card can indicate that you are out of your league. Accepting restrictions or disappointments with decency is a good thing to do.

Love: You may be attempting to adjust as rapidly as possible. Confusion and unrest will occur as a result of this. It is good to listen to your mind and heart, but it's also a good idea to be open to new ideas and attempt to understand things from the other person's point of view. Instead of trying to get your way, seek understanding.

Career: Before you evolve, you need to first listen and understand. You may become puzzled and consequently, hesitate to act or decide on issues. Indecisiveness has led to missed opportunities and failures; now is the moment to understand your limitations. Look for clarity and stay away from the problems of others. It is not a good time to make enemies.

Six of Swords

Element: Air

Astrological signs: Gemini, Libra, Aquarius

Upright: Good going, respectful, jaunting

Reversed: Drags feet, coward, no progress

Card description: The illustration on the Six of Swords depicts a mother and her child sitting in a boat. A person is rowing them across the water to land on the opposite side of the body of water. Because the woman and the child are pictured with their backs turned to us, we can deduce that they are escaping from something or someone. A cloak covers the woman's head. It is possible that she's trying to run away from something, and she needs to do so without anyone else discovering who she really is. We can reasonably assume that she is going through a period of profound loss or sadness. The Six of Swords can represent either a loss or a change in one's circumstances, as well as the beginning of a journey towards a future that holds more potential than the one we have left in the past. Compared to intuition and the heart, the rational mind possesses a strong power, symbolised by the six swords standing on the boat.

Number association: The sixes, in contrast to the fives, which indicate conflict, symbolise the transition from that conflict into a resolution, whether it be internal or external, whether it includes reconciliation or letting go. They represent the triumph over adversity and the dawning of light.

Personal growth: This card represents clarity of mind and a sense of comprehension. With the support of your knowledge, you can go a long way. The time is ripe to begin a physical or spiritual adventure. All your experiences will lead to enlightenment, which

cases, people have the urge to leave their present circumstances without offending or harming others they once cared about. They are tricky with hazy motivations. Those who are unfamiliar with them might think they are unpredictable. As a result, some people can find it challenging to approach the Seven of Swords since their enigmatic aura makes casual confrontation too daunting. But those who meet them can be rewarded by meeting an intriguing and complex individual.

Money: It is time to think for yourself when it comes to money. You can earn money using your history, networks and expertise. You may explore elsewhere, if you find a position with many constraints that do not suit your criteria. A negative mindset may hamper prosperity and growth. This card also signifies a turning point in your life.

Love: Raise your voice for what you believe is right and do not let others make all the decisions. Try to be diplomatic rather than get into a dispute with your partner. Compromise is the best option. If it is not possible, look for a partner who will let you have free thought and with whom you can communicate your feelings.

Career: Your main feature is mental openness and creativity. If your current job does not provide you with these two benefits, you should look for another job. Other plans may require alteration. You must avoid direct conflict and disagreements.

cases, people have the urge to leave their present circumstances without offending or harming others they once cared about. They are tricky with hazy motivations. Those who are unfamiliar with them might think they are unpredictable. As a result, some people can find it challenging to approach the Seven of Swords since their enigmatic aura makes casual confrontation too daunting. But those who meet them can be rewarded by meeting an intriguing and complex individual.

Money: It is time to think for yourself when it comes to money. You can earn money using your history, networks and expertise. You may explore elsewhere, if you find a position with many constraints that do not suit your criteria. A negative mindset may hamper prosperity and growth. This card also signifies a turning point in your life.

Love: Raise your voice for what you believe is right, and do not let others make all the decisions. Try to be diplomatic rather than get into a dispute with your partner. Compromise is the best option. If it is not possible, look for a partner who will let you have free thought and with whom you can communicate your feelings.

Career: All you require is mental openness and creativity. If your current job does not provide you with these two benefits, you should look for another job. Other plans may require alteration. You must avoid direct conflict and disagreements.

Eight of Swords

Element: Air

Astrological signs: Gemini, Libra, Aquarius

Upright: Bondage, fear, voiceless

Reversed: Escape, healing, mental strength

Card description: The Eight of Swords card depicts a blindfolded woman in restraints. Eight swords are strategically placed around, restricting her movement. It seems as though she is in a cage or prison. It also appears that the person responsible for tying her up was careless or rushed, as they left a gap through which she could flee. But since the woman cannot see because she is wearing a blindfold, she is unable to find a way to free herself from this snare. The desolate landscape that surrounds her may be symbolic of an absence of creativity of some kind, while the cloudy sky seen in the background may be symbolic of despair because she believes that there is no chance of her escaping her circumstances. If only she could remove the blindfold, she would realise that she is free to leave this predicament at any time by simply walking away.

Number association: The eights signify the end of a second phase and typically represent some form of accomplishment, whether it be materialistic or emotional. Here, growth may be in both directions, and it occasionally manifests itself in ways that we least expect.

Personal growth: You are your own worst enemy you have ever had. This card asks you to let go of your self-limiting mindset impeding your growth. Let go of your doubts and worries, and have faith in the plan of the universe.

harm their self-assurance and self-esteem. These obsessions have the potential to induce stagnation, which is incredibly destructive to their ability to form new relationships and advance in their careers.

Money: Money-related issues can cause feelings of despair, remorse, anxiety, and worry. You will suffer losses because of your refusal to confront reality for far too long. These losses, on the other hand, may lighten the load you have been holding. The card also indicates that you are only considering the negative aspects of your situation.

Love: The card depicts a terrible scenario caused by another person's insensitivity. It is easy to feel isolated, ignored and abandoned. You have let someone else define you or have chosen to ignore the truth about yourself or your spouse. Deal with this situation with understanding and try to make sense of what happened and how to minimise repeating the same mistakes in the future.

Career: The nine implies that negativity and worry are to blame for your lack of success. You may blame others for your mistakes or let them decide what you should do. Rather than harping on or sobbing about problems, you should address the reality for yourself and your aspirations.

harm their self-assurance and self-esteem. These obsessions have the potential to induce stagnation, which is incredibly destructive to their ability to form new relationships and advance in their careers.

Money: Money-related issues can cause feelings of despair, remorse, anxiety, and worry. You will suffer losses because of your refusal to confront reality for far too long. These losses, on the other hand, may lighten the load you have been holding. The card also indicates that you are only considering the negative aspects of your situation.

Love: The card depicts a terrible scenario caused by another person's insensitivity. It is easy to feel isolated, ignored and abandoned. You have let someone else define you or have chosen to ignore the truth about yourself or your spouse. Deal with this situation with understanding and try to make sense of what happened and how to minimise repeating the same mistakes in the future.

Career: The nine implies that negativity and worry are to blame for your lack of success. You may blame others for your mistakes or let them decide what you should do. Rather than focusing on or sobbing about problems, you should address the reality for yourself and your aspirations.

Ten of Swords

Element: Air

Astrological signs: Gemini, Libra, Aquarius

Upright: Enmity, destroyed, wreck

Reversed: Surviving, dealing with issues, improvement

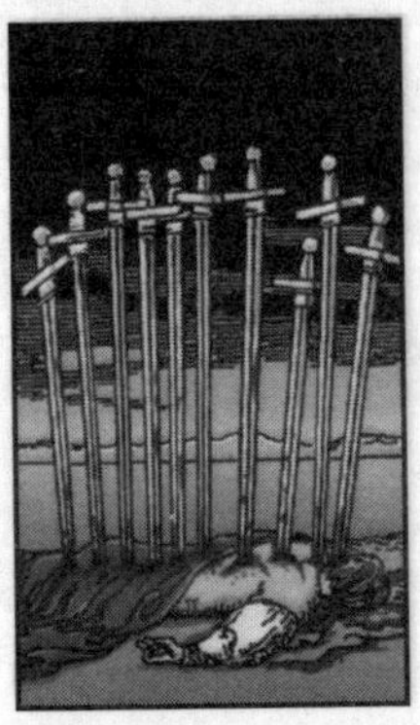

Card description: The Ten of Swords depicts a man lying face down on the ground and is one of the deck's most distinctive and unsettling cards. He is draped in a crimson blanket from his chest to his knees. He might not have seen this ending coming as ten long swords are thrust into his back. The sky above him is dark and cloudy, symbolising the fear and negativity that comes with death, and there is a terrible stillness in the air. The sea is calm, adding to the sense of finality and calmness. The sun rises over the eastern horizon, indicating hope. The Ten of Swords suggests that this is the absolute bottom of the barrel and that there is no way to go lower. Despite everything, the sun is on its upward journey.

Number association: In the tens, we see the actual end of the cycle, that something has come full circle; this denotes that we can head towards a fresh start.

Personal growth: The card represents knowledge obtained through adversity. It is time you took care of your health, as you are probably physically fatigued. Allow yourself some rest because you are overworked and exhausted.

About a person: The Ten of Swords, as a person, is dramatic, and for who defeat, no matter how small or big, is perceived as the end of the world. They can be prone to exaggerating their difficulties; one sword becomes ten. The Ten of Swords has

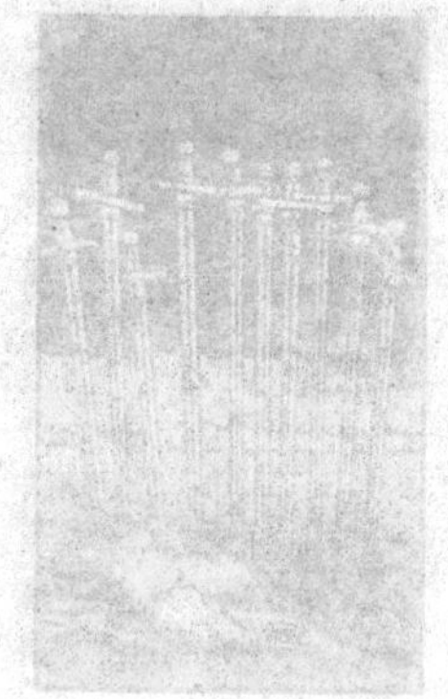

Love: Observe the partnership of your partner to acquire a better understanding. Someone is keeping an eye on you, so stay vigilant. The card represents a distanced, immature, and analytical relationship style. Instead of experiencing love, you and your spouse will only talk about it. It is essential to have effective communication channels.

Career: Establish your own thinking and avoid ideas of others. Develop your own abilities to become successful. The card warns you that someone you may interact with is potentially untrustworthy.

Knight of Swords

Element: Air

Astrological Signs: Gemini, Libra, Aquarius

Upright: Audacious, wisp, humorous

Reversed: Careless, undue haste, adamant.

Card description: That knight sure is in a hurry! Card number eleven from the Major Arcana, Knight of Swords, shows a young man in full battle gear, mounted on a stalwart white horse, charging headfirst into the fray. The white horse symbolises the young man's pristine mental state and boundless drive. The background depicts storm clouds and trees, blown around wildly by strong winds. The horse's harness is embellished with pictures of flora and fauna. It is worth noting that those same birds also appear on the knight's cape.

Possible events: Arguments may happen. No one will support you. Everyone seems to neglect and disrespect you, and you may feel lonely.

Love: Observe the partnership or your partner to acquire a better understanding. Someone is keeping an eye on you, so stay vigilant. The card represents a distanced, immature, and analytical relationship style. Instead of experiencing love, you and your spouse will only talk about it. It is essential to have effective communication channels.

Career: Establish your own thinking and avoid ideas of others. Develop your own abilities to become successful. The card warns you that someone you may interact with is potentially untrustworthy.

Knight of Swords

Element: Air

Astrological signs: Gemini, Libra, Aquarius

Upright: Audacious, wise, humorous

Reversed: Careless, undue haste, adamant

Card description: That knight sure is in a hurry. Card number eleven from the Major Arcana, Knight of Swords, shows a young man in full battle gear, mounted on a stalwart white horse, charging headfirst into the fray. The white horse symbolises the young man's pristine mental state and boundless drive. The background depicts storm clouds and trees, blown around wildly by strong winds. The horse's harness is embellished with pictures of flora and fauna. It is worth noting that those same birds also appear on the knight's cape.

Possible events: Arguments may happen. No one will support you. Everyone seems to neglect and disrespect you, and you may feel lonely.

Personal growth: You must alter your viewpoint, mindset and knowledge. Rather than removing barriers to safeguard your weakness, become more dynamic and adaptive.

About a person: The Knight of Swords, as a person, is someone who enjoys the chance to make decisive judgements. You are a strong person who can make challenging decisions seem simple. Your determination to move forward has caught the attention of others around you, even if you still have much to learn about the advantages of careful consideration. You are popular in society thanks to your charm and quick wit. You do not see yourself as a natural leader and the protagonist of a bigger story. You do not value humility.

Money: You may believe you know everything, yet failing to listen to others might cost you a lot. This card can also indicate a sudden change in your income. It is time for a change in your business or other financial areas. You will probably go on a trip concerning business or wealth-related matters.

Love: Usually, the card refers to transformation. There is a chance that an existing relationship may terminate or that a new romance will begin. However, you must be more adaptable and corporative. Try to break old related behaviours. Try not to be too harsh with your partner.

Career: There is a chance that your workplace culture, occupation or duties will change. Change your mindset and the way you conduct your job by becoming more enthusiastic and open-minded. Conflicts should be discouraged. Greater control and aim can help you work to excel more. The card could also indicate a business trip soon or a career that requires travel.

Queen of Swords

Element: Air

Astrological signs: Gemini, Libra, Aquarius

Upright: Wise, loves freedom, discern

Reversed: Insincere, deceit, pungent

QUEEN of SWORDS.

Card description: The Queen of Swords sits erect on her throne, decorated with cherubs and butterflies. She stares into the distance. Queen of the element of air that the swords represent, her lofty perch above the clouds demonstrates that she can't be manipulated or deceived. The blade of her right-hand sword is raised to the heavens, while the palm of her left hand is outstretched as if she were offering a gift. The Queen of Swords bestows the ability to use our discretion in making day-to-day choices and the adaptability to take in new information from others.

Possible events: You need to fight against tremendous odds to taste success. In return, you will get only criticism.

Personal growth: The Queen is a clear symbol of intelligence that prevailed over feelings. Be more reasonable and clear-headed by putting away all emotional or selfish feelings. It's time for you to seize control of your fate. Allowing people to make your decision for you is not a good idea.

About a person: The Queen of Swords, as a person, possesses an intuitive sense of intelligence and is a quick thinker. She is also a formidable opponent. Their ability to reason exceeds their emotional state. She is an excellent example. When the Queen of Swords occurs in a spread, it indicates that the person possesses mental clarity that permeates all aspects of their day-to-day existence. They can comprehend events clearly and see beyond emotional barriers, which contributes to developing a rational worldview predominated by logical reasoning in their thinking.

Money: The card suggests you make money using your data and communication technology. Take control of your financial situation and turn it around. Try not to get involved in any dubious transactions, as losses may occur.

Love: You may believe that your current circumstance is too constraining and is tying you to tradition. It is time to talk with your thoughts and take a hard stance if you want to attain your desires. Keep it simple and basic. Maintain a distant and rational mindset while controlling your emotions. The Queen also indicates that you are feeling detached or in charge.

Career: Get a clear picture of what you want and then speak up. You will feel restricted and need to exert control in a task issue. The card also denotes a job in information technology or communications, which can provide productive outcomes.

King of Swords

Element: Air

Astrological signs: Gemini, Libra, Aquarius

Upright: Thoughtful, dominating, intellect

Reversed: Browbeat others, manipulative, bias

Card description: The King of Swords tarot card shows a monarch seated on a throne with an double-edged sword in his right hand pointing up. The throne is decorated with butterflies, crescent moons and an angel. Change is represented by the butterflies. The king's blue tunic symbolises his enlightened mind; and the purple cape, his intellect.

The intellectual authority of the King of Swords is shown in his sharp mind, impeccable judgement, and unwavering commitment to the truth. He recognises the gravity of his newfound authority.

Possible events: Always proactive but at times dominated by others also.

Personal growth: Develop your mental abilities and use your knowledge to gain a grip on the situation. By concentrating on this card, you will be able to strengthen your mind and reasoning thinking.

About a person: The King of Swords, as a person, is composed, austere and assertive, and always prefers the truth to his gut feeling. Individuals symbolised by this card rarely make snap judgements. They instead prefer to examine the advantages and disadvantages of every circumstance. The rationality that governs the King of Swords' daily activities is seen in his rigidly scheduled routine. These routine tasks serve to an end. If the King of Swords is you, then they are essential to helping you reach the precise objectives you have set for yourself. You detest being inactive and believe you perform at your best when working on worthwhile projects. You are happiest when working towards a definite objective, whether this involves eating healthily, exercising, wearing nicely, or moving up the social ladder. You are a disciplined and focused worker who does a great job. You might discover that you are drawn to powerful positions where you can organise and mobilise sizeable numbers of people for a specific goal.

Money: Act decisively rather than hesitating. It is time to take charge. Take control of your circumstances and finances by utilising everything you know. It is not the time to expose your sources or knowledge at this time. Stay detached, and do not let your emotions rule you. You can make profits by investing in the sphere of information.

Love: The relationship will be based on communicative concepts and ideas, rather than genuine sentiments. You and your partner have high values, but you both engage in an outdated and disconnected manner. You may be afraid that if you fall in love, you will lose control or freedom. You talk about and think about love, but you will resist the emotion.

Career: The King foreshadows a job or vocation that involves communication or creative skills. Decisiveness and objectivity are required. It's also a good idea to demonstrate your ability to lead. At this point, it's critical to remain focused and clear. It's crucial to understand with whom you're sharing your data. Don't give up until you get the answers you want.

Suit of Pentacles (Coin)

With the earth as its element, its unfolding light covers objective gains. This suit probably answers all your queries related to money.

Upright position of Pentacles indicates dignity, winner, potent wealth, firmness.

Reversed position of Pentacles indicates an insatiable desire of wealth, money stuck, love for non-living things over living.

Ace of Pentacles

Element: Earth

Astrological signs: Virgo, Capricorn, Taurus

Upright: Name and fame, handsome bank balance, surety

Reversed: Counterfeit, mean, avarice

Card description: A single, enigmatic hand materialises from the sky in this card. The object in the hand resembles a gold coin with a pentagram engraved on it. This pentacle represents prosperity and earthly goods, as the earth is a symbol of the element associated with it. The garden below the hand gives off an air of growth, prosperity and fertility thanks to its abundance of flowers and other plant life. The mountain is a metaphor for the ambition needed to pursue the pentacle. The ebb and flow of the creek suggest that the protagonist's feelings are also moving towards achieving this goal.

Number association: You'll know when something new with a lot of potential is coming if your readings contain a lot of aces. They are merely formless pure energy, and it is up to you to mould them and materialise the potential they stand for. They are unstable because they are raw, and if you don't take care, they can overwhelm you very soon.

Personal growth: You can deal with practical issues with ease. The card advises you to take care of your health as well. Start meditating on this card if you want to become more anchored and realistic.

About a person: The Ace of Pentacles, as a person, is financially savvy, career-minded, and concerned for their personal well-being, as well as the well-being of those in their immediate environment. They want to avoid confrontation as far as possible, but when confronted with it, they will not back down. When they invest their attention and energy into something that they value, they are highly focused and, as a result, they often achieve their goals.

Money: The Ace in business refers to a new commercial venture, financing, or other monetary achievement. You will likely be given the opportunity to earn money. This is the ideal time to lay the groundwork. Attempt any new ventures cautiously, as the results will be positive.

Love: There is a good chance you will meet a loving companion at work who is financially or materially stable. The card demonstrates that you should approach a new alliance with a practical and grounded approach. It may also point to the early stages of a physical attraction-based relationship.

Career: In terms of work, project, or company, the Ace represents a fresh start. In addition, you may be able to obtain financial assistance to go on an adventure. You must put in a lot of effort if you want your new business to succeed.

Two of Pentacles

Element: Earth

Astrological signs: Virgo, Capricorn, Taurus

Upright: Good luck, good perception, travelling

Reversed: Realm of problems, not uniform, perturbed

Card description: The man on the Two of Pentacles dances while balancing two large coins. The infinity symbol that encircles the pentacles is a symbol of the ability of the man to deal with whatever challenges life throws at him. Two ships cruise on the enormous waves in the background, emphasising the precariousness of the situation. The Two of Pentacles portrays the ups and downs of everyday life. The man seems unconcerned by his chaotic environment; he dances and accepts whatever life throws at him with a positive attitude.

Number association: The topic of the twos is pairing up, with all the complications that this union entails. We go from the oneness, and the twos offer a glimpse of togetherness. The twos typically stand for harmony and the coming together of opposing elements to form a whole. This harmony can occasionally be so flawless that it makes it impossible to move on and causes paralysis when we need to decide.

Personal growth: When the situation involves physical or practical problems, the card indicates a period of discomfort and doubt. This is the ideal moment to work on your abilities. It may also take some time for you to recognise how far you have come. It is critical to concentrate on both the process and the end goal.

About a person: The Two of Pentacles, as a person, represents someone who can confidently handle whatever new hell life decides to hurl at them. They understand that taking significant risks is required to accomplish one's objectives. As they can readily adapt to anything life throws at them, good or bad, they are not scared to take those risks. With Jupiter as their astrological significator, they tend to be lucky but risk losing everything they have achieved. They are often kind-hearted and endowed with a dry, sarcastic sense of humour that helps them through difficult situations. It may come as no surprise that they frequently enjoy sarcasm and dark humour.

Money: The Two of Pentacles represent a period of early progress on a financial or physical level. Do not make any large changes or expect significant outcomes. Money may come in and out quickly, requiring you to manage it. The card also represents two distinct money streams.

Love: Because you may be irritable or restless in your relationship, you should seek some alterations and reassess what you desire at this time. You and your companion should divide your commitments and financial issues. The Two of Pentacles also symbolises the sharing of resources.

Career: Insecurity and instability can arise due to changes in your employment or work environment. You will be impatient as well because you won't notice any progress. Balance your time, labour and assets. The Two of Pentacles also denotes two employments or two ways of obtaining money.

Three of Pentacles

Element: Earth

Astrological signs: Virgo, Capricorn, Taurus

Upright: Renown, together, achiever

Reversed: Postpone, controversy, harsh

Card description: The Three of Pentacles depicts a young apprentice in a cathedral. He is working with his tools. He looks up to see a priest and an aristocrat holding the cathedral's blueprints on parchment. The two seem to be offering their knowledge and opinions so they can guide him. The two master builders pay attention to the apprentice, even though the latter has less experience because they recognise that the apprentice's insights and knowledge are crucial to the overall success of the building project. The Three of Pentacles, then, symbolises the synthesis of varied fields of expertise into a cohesive whole.

Number association: The tarot's threes are governed by group dynamics, and they represent many events that might happen when groups of people or ideas join. It also denotes an initial completion of a first phase of some kind because it is also conceptualised symbolically as completion (the first polygon, the Holy Trinity, etc.).

Personal growth: This is the artisan's card, combining both creativity and pragmatism. The card defines the process of putting your ideas and talents to good use. It also denotes the end of a stage in your own development. You should meditate on this card if you wish your dreams to come true.

About a person: The Three of Pentacles, as a person, typically represents those that flourish in teams, have strong communication abilities, and enjoy their work much. They frequently have positions that entail manual labour, such as those in construction, but also hold occupations closely related to real estate, such as agent, mortgage broker, or loan officer. They are noted for their honesty and ability to solve problems; they don't give up quickly. Nonetheless, they are kind and excellent listeners when assisting others.

Money: You can make money by investing your energy, skill set, and assets. This card indicates that a stage of a financial undertaking has been completed successfully. The card also advises you to improve your talents to boost your earnings.

Love: The Three of Pentacles can represent a period for retribution. It could be the moment to see how your efforts will soon manifest. It could be the time to finally appreciate each other and discover happiness as you overcome the hurdles.

Career: The Three of Pentacles represents the constructive use of your ability to achieve a lasting physical outcome. It is time to look at other options for monetising your hard work and talent. You might also look for a job that enables you to develop and expand your knowledge. According to the card, you will complete a project successfully or end work on good terms.

Four of Pentacles

Element: Earth

Astrological signs: Virgo, Capricorn, Taurus

Upright: Happiness, strong wealthy background

Reversed: Avarice, irresolution, love for objects

Card description: This card depicts a man seated on a stool and adopting a very defensive and tense posture while holding onto a coin. The man is associated with the suit of defence. It is almost as if he's trying to keep hold of them all for fear of losing them. One of the pentacles is perched perilously on top of his head, another is held firmly in both of his hands, and the remaining two are tucked away safely beneath his feet. He is taking extreme precautions to ensure no one can take his coins. At the same time, he cannot move as he has clenched the coins. His actions are restricted because he is clinging on to his possessions. He does not seem to have any friends or family. He is fixated on wealth.

Number association: The number four typically denotes the establishment of a foundation. The goal here is to grow and evolve since, even if the foundation has been laid, there may occasionally be some disappointment because things may not have gone exactly as planned. The fours are therefore another way that the universe is encouraging us to advance and flourish.

Personal growth: The card advises that you use your imagination to put your ideas into action in a reliable manner. It is time to figure out your worth and start looking for stability within yourself. By meditating on this card, you can boost yourself.

About a person: The Four of Pentacles, as a person, typically represents individuals driven by money and material prosperity.

Although they often believe they are smarter, more attractive, and superior to most of those around them, they can be obstinate and difficult to deal with. Despite their varied talents and unwavering drive, they are frequently domineering and stubborn, resistant to the counsel their friends and family offer them, and far less successful in their interpersonal relationships than they are in their financial endeavours.

Money: The Four of Pentacles signify the formation and accumulation of resources and money. It is safe to say that you're saving wisely and have a solid financial foundation. In some circumstances, this card also indicates that an investment of yours is sound. It also implies that you are concerned about money and security.

Love: On the one hand, the card clearly depicts a loyal and stable partner, as well as a partnership; on the other hand, it can also depict a relationship that has grown overly organised and now lacks thrill or freedom. In certain circumstances, the card clearly represents a connection focused on security and money.

Career: The Four of Pentacles indicates that your job condition is steady and you are financially secure. It also says your abilities are highly respected, allowing you to earn a nice living. You may be aware that you are into this profession not because you enjoy it, but because it provides you security. The Four of Pentacles also represents the fact that status and power are by-products of money.

Five of Pentacles

Element: Earth

Astrological signs: Virgo, Capricorn, Taurus

Upright: Hardship, no income, end of savings

Reversed: Overcoming adversity, forgiveness, change

Card description: The Five of Pentacles, like the other suits' fives, represents difficulty. Two people are walking outside in the snow. They are not only cold but ill, poor, tired, and hungry as well. It appears that they are struggling to provide for even the most fundamental needs. Many people will find at least one way in which they can identify with both characters.

The figures in the card wear scarves, and one uses crutches. Amidst the snow, she chooses to go shoeless. A stained-glass window depicting the five pentacles decorates a black wall in the background, which may be part of a church.

The Five of Pentacles is a bad omen in most cases. Not to worry, though; its meaning shifts depending on context.

Number association: The fives stand for transition, change, turbulence, and strife (at times). The fives come after the fours and amplify the same energy. The fives encourage us to seek within for a deeper cause for why to move forward when that energy explodes. We must advance to overcome this instability and move forward.

Personal growth: The number five is immediately associated with a waste of time, resources, and skill set. Don't correlate worth with money or possessions. Instead, focus on improving yourself from the inside out. Whatever you give up monetarily now will pay out in the long run spiritually.

About a person: The Five of Pentacles, as a person, is frequently an outcast and one of society's less fortunate individuals. They may lack fortune in life, make little money, and have few, if any, chances to improve things and prosper. This frequently encourages a pattern of negativity towards oneself and several facets of one's life. Although they are aware that something important is lacking in their life, they are unable to make any changes. They frequently feel overwhelmed and need assistance from others to survive.

Money: Five of Pentacles has been linked to poverty and scarcity. However, it also denotes freedom from the responsibilities that come with wealth and property. It simply indicates that you should place a greater emphasis on spiritual matters rather than money matters. Making your living as simple as possible is advised. It is also a good idea to restrict your personal items to what is extremely necessary. Now is not the time to obtain a return on an investment you are about to make.

Love: This is an excellent moment to let go of anyone or anything that causes you emotional, creative, or bodily stress. Do not be answerable to anyone, and stick to it. It is preferable to be alone and appreciated.

Career: This card shows that you may not be earning enough money at your current employment. You are under stress because of your work responsibilities. You are also not putting your skills to good use at work. This card also suggests that you are not getting the recognition you deserve. It is time to start looking for a new job.

Six of Pentacles

Element: Earth

Astrological signs: Virgo, Capricorn, Taurus

Upright: Donation, rising profit, stability

Reversed: Extravagant, money setback, inequality

Card description: The Six of Pentacles depicts a man in a robe. His appearance represents the man's wealth and high social standing. In one hand, he holds a scale, representing fairness and equality. The Justice tarot card comes to mind and reminds us of karma, cause and effect, and the idea that we get back in life what we give. He is distributing coins to two beggars kneeling at his feet. The Six of Pentacles indicates that you are financially stable enough to help others without jeopardising your own situation.

Number Association: The sixes, in contrast to the fives, which indicate conflict, symbolise the transition from that conflict into a resolution, whether internal or external, or whether it includes reconciliation or letting go. They represent the triumph over adversity and the dawning of light.

Personal growth: You should understand the importance of giving and receiving. Allow others to support you and be willing to help them in return. Start being fairer with your energy, capabilities, and other things if you want people to be good to you.

About a person: The Six of Pentacles, as a person, is a highly vibrant individual. They are often dependable and robust, making other people envious of their strong aura. The Six of Pentacles has a strong sense of community and will do whatever it takes to support their friends and family. They have learnt to be calm and patient through their spiritual connection, and they constantly strive to do kind things for the benefit of others.

Money: This card reveals your prosperity and willingness to share your possessions. This is the perfect time to start a financial endeavour and collaborate with others. Both parties will gain from these activities. This is the perfect moment to associate with people in order to boost your revenues. A monetary gift is on its way for you.

Love: Now is a crucial time to give and take. You must share your financial resources with your partner to prosper together. The card also denotes a money-making or business-related enterprise with a romantic partner, and you must be receptive to what the other person is presenting to you.

Career: Number six is associated with group projects, corporate relationships, and collaboration. You should share your resources and responsibilities with all those people whose abilities and assets complement yours in order to be successful. You will get a fantastic opportunity to work with others on a noteworthy project or business.

Seven of Pentacles

Element: Earth

Astrological signs: Virgo, Capricorn, Taurus

Upright: Determined, good way of working, ultimate

Reversed: Lost chances, hopeless, lending money to deceitful people

Card description: The young man depicted on the Seven of Pentacles appears to be taking some time off from his labour to enjoy the bounty of his garden. He sets his shovel down and leans back to take in the seven pentacles that dangle from the verdant foliage above him. The way he rests his head on the shovel indicates that he is tired; he has laboured diligently to ensure that this year's harvest will be successful. One of the pentacles is at his feet, but he chooses to save the rest because he is more concerned with the long-term than with enjoying his current bounty. He plans on cultivating his harvest for the long haul with his efforts.

Number association: When there are several sevens in a reading, it typically means that it's time to take a step back and reflect. The sevens challenge us to rethink and assess whether we are on the right course and is the best one for us. Although it can occasionally feel lonely, this phase is necessary if you want to go forward with your true desires.

Personal growth: Despite putting in a great deal of effort, the result is still not apparent. Do not be concerned or discouraged. Continue honing your skill at your own pace. If you truly want to improve your patience, the best method to do it is to meditate on this card.

About a person: The Seven of Pentacles, as a person, does not take the time to enjoy life. No matter how much time and dedication they devote to a project, they still feel they have not put enough effort into it. They believe that the key to success is never taking a break. On the plus side, persons embodied by the Seven of Pentacles are extremely perseverant and regularly sow seeds that will blossom years from now.

Money: It is not a favourable time for you to get results, so do not rush things. Instead, be patient and persistent. It is also a good idea not to lose faith during this period, even if the progress is gradual and consistent. Do not fall into money-making schemes or anything that appears too good to be true.

Love: If you do not feel like you are making much progress or your relationship isn't going as well as you would want, this card tells you to be patient. You should take little measures toward your goals and continue to work on them. You have a long way to go before you arrive at your destination.

Career: This is the perfect time to exercise patience and perseverance in any activity you are attempting. This is the time to pay close attention to details and give it your all. Now is the moment to put all your effort and resources into achieving your goal. It is safe to assume that the effort you put in today will bear fruit tomorrow.

Eight of Pentacles

Element: Earth

Astrological signs: Virgo, Capricorn, Taurus

Upright: Luck favours you, artistic, contentment

Reversed: Aimless, closed doors for yourself, lazy

Card description: The Eight of Pentacles shows a young man carving a pentacle pattern into a stack of eight golden coins. The person depicted on the card is engrossed in his action. The town in the background indicates that he has successfully removed himself from potential distractions. In the context of the tarot, the Eight of Pentacles represents times when you put in extra effort to get something done. You have thrown yourself into the task at hand, and you are determined to submit a polished final product.

Number association: The eights signify the end of a second phase and typically represent some form of accomplishment, whether it is materialistic or emotional. Here, growth may be in both directions, and it occasionally manifests itself in ways we least expect.

Personal growth: Continue to work hard to reach perfection. Keep your gaze and focus solely on your goal, and work diligently to attain it. You must not take any shortcuts and study as much as possible. This card may also counsel that you pay attention to your health and seek to improve it.

About a person: The Eight of Pentacles, as a person, is exceedingly diligent, devoted and committed. He may hold a junior job or is new to the company. This person, who may be a learner of some kind, is drawn to the exciting beginnings of a project when there is a lot of reading and studying involved.

This type of person may become fixated on things that don't seem relevant to those around them and may lose sight of the big picture. Building a relationship with or even gaining the trust of the Eight of Pentacles takes time.

Money: You may have to spend money to earn money since money attracts money. This card advises you to put out all your efforts and go to any lengths necessary to achieve your financial objectives. Devote your time and effort to a financial business. In other circumstances, the number eight also implies that additional knowledge is required before you can start making money.

Love: If you want your relationship to be successful, you should put in sufficient effort. You should begin offering more love in your life to obtain more love. This is a chance for you to grow and learn. Relationships, like every other area of life, require effort in order to thrive. The number eight can also signify the arrival of passion late in life.

Career: The need of the hour is to apply yourself and master your abilities. You may also be required to devote yourself entirely to your task for some time. You must also acquire more skills and information in a highly defined field. Set realistic objectives for yourself and work hard to become the best version of yourself.

Nine of Pentacles

Element: Earth

Astrological signs: Virgo, Capricorn, Taurus

Upright: Objective gain, winner, socially alone

Reversed: Cheat, to and fro motion of money, reckless

Card description: A woman stands in the centre of a vineyard on the Nine of Pentacles. The woman wears a voluminous, expensive dress with sunflowers as decoration. She appears wealthy; a castle is in the background. She has a falcon perched on her left hand, where it is relaxing and playing. The golden coins and plump grapes on the vines behind her represent her bountiful harvest representing the fruitful accomplishment of her efforts.

Number association: The nines suggest close to completion, which could mean reaching a plateau. What appears to be the finish line might be a temporary stage. Even though there is a sense of finality, this is typically just a brief period before the cycle's conclusion.

Personal growth: You may have complete control over your powers and possessions. This is feasible because you recognise your own worth and significance. It is an excellent moment to put your financial knowledge and skills to good use by assisting others.

About a person: The Nine of Pentacles, as a person, typically depicts a female individual. Number nine denotes the end of a cycle; this woman may be approaching menopause and slowing down or about to experience a fresh beginning with a kid and pregnancy. She carries herself with dignity and is independent and self-assured. She enjoys the fine things in life and does not worry about money because her labour of love has allowed her to enjoy the luxuries. She spends a lot of time outside and takes good care of herself.

Money: This card depicts both physical and financial well-being. This is the time to celebrate your achievements. It is the time when you will get handsome rewards for all your hard work. Make good use of your resources, and you will reap the rewards. It is the ideal moment to pay off any debt you may have accumulated.

Love: Regarding relationships, the Nine of Pentacles card represents contentment and security. It is time to savour the delights you've earned while battling storms and other adversities. Number nine also represents a partnership that delivers not only physical fulfilment, but also financial abundance.

Career: The card states that you will be recognised and appreciated for your efforts and hard work. If you take control of your job, you will eventually attain a position of leadership. Others will respect your accomplishments and abilities as a result of this. It is always preferable to gain great success with your own efforts and abilities. Congratulations, you have worked hard for your success, and now is the time to enjoy it.

Ten of Pentacles

Element: Earth

Astrological signs: Virgo, Capricorn, Taurus

Upright: Strong sentiments, peaceful abode, money, heritage

Reversed: Dispute with kin, fiscal blockage, instability

Card description: The Ten of Pentacles depicts an old man reclining in an entrance archway to a sprawling mansion. Many younger relatives surround him, suggesting he is the family patriarch. Grapevines and crescent moons adorn his robe, representing the union of spirit and matter. The man is surrounded by his loved ones and pets. A smiling couple, likely his kids, stand directly in front of him, and a young boy or girl, probably his grandchild, plays behind them. The child makes a joyful attempt to play with the dog.

Number association: In the tens, we see the actual end of the cycle, that something has come full circle; this denotes that moving forward, we can head towards a fresh start.

Personal growth: Ten denotes a great sense of self-worth, security and inner strength. All these characteristics can only come from a family that supports you in any scenario or from your own efforts to succeed. Your personal strength can inspire others. By meditating on this card, you can strengthen your inner security and self-confidence.

About a person: He is worn-out but content, and wrinkles surround his eyes. The old man portrayed on the Ten of Pentacles has accomplished great things, and he is now relishing the fruits of his labour as he looks around at his children and grandchildren. His pride beams as he sees them. The Ten of Pentacles represents someone who has had a successful career and is financially independent. People consulted them when they have to take significant decisions because they are respected members of their community or family, especially when those decisions require a sizeable financial commitment.

Money: This card is a strong representation of wealth and property. There are more possibilities of receiving inherited or family money for personal use. It is an auspicious moment for prosperity and riches. The card also suggests that you invest in large-scale initiatives or charitable endeavours.

Love: The Ten of Pentacles denotes completion, security and contentment. It is the time when a partner can step up to help you develop your talents while bolstering your sense of self-worth and work. The themes for this card are family and home, implying that you are now preparing to start a family of your own. In certain situations, the conclusion reveals marriage into a family of prestige and wealth.

Career: Ten of Pentacles card implies external success. Name and renown might be yours because you have all the necessary skills to achieve more. This is the moment to apply your skills and assets by engaging in charitable projects or working on larger projects.

Page of Pentacles

Element: Earth

Astrological signs: Virgo, Capricorn, Taurus

Upright: Great effort, respectful, honest

Reversed: Lethargic, covetous, short-tempered

Card description: A young man stands alone in a field filled with flowers on the Page of Pentacles card. There are some dense trees and a furrowed field in the background. The young man seems to be oblivious to his surroundings; his focus is clearly on the coin in his hand and all the ideas it symbolises, including success, safety, wealth, beauty in nature and sexuality. The Page of Pentacles represents someone reliable, hard-working and rooted in reality.

Possible events: Be circumspect, spend money wisely, and look after your savings. Some surprises in terms of money are waiting for you.

Personal growth: You should attend to practical things and keep track of all the minutiae of your life. You may be required to help others or carry out a mission. The card expressly states that now is the time to pay attention to your health.

About a person: The Page of Pentacles, as a person, is a realistic, accountable, and conscientious person in his personal life. Although they lack experience, they have a lot of promise and are maturing quickly. When the Page of Pentacles have to complete a job or a project, they give it their undivided attention and carefully analyse all their choices before taking action. Individuals whose cards include the Page of Pentacles are at the start of their travels and have big aspirations for the years to come. They will put it into action.

Money: This card represents matters about money. You must thoroughly examine financial paperwork and investments. It is also critical and recommended that you memorise all your financial affairs. You demonstrate your practical skills and avoid letting sentiments sway your financial choices.

Love: This card shows a straightforward, down-to-earth approach to a relationship. This card reflects the partner's description, which is less romantic and exciting and focuses on realistic or ordinary matters.

Career: This card represents working in a practical profession or a support role and could be a health-related topic or attribute. It could also be a sign of an entry-level job or training. Your work provides financial security but is lacking in zest and vibrancy. Compared to self-expression or popularity, stability and money are more significant.

Knight of Pentacles

Element: Earth

Astrological signs: Virgo, Capricorn, Taurus

Upright: Hard-headed, diligent, honest

Reversed: Lousy, not looking to improve, excessive desires

Card description: The Knight of Pentacles, like the other court cards comprising the suit, emphasises diligence, hard work, and taking on one's fair share of responsibilities. On a field, the Knight of Pentacles rides a dark horse. Rather than joining his fellow knights on their constant quests, he has chosen to stay and work. The ploughed fields indicate that he has worked hard to realise his dreams. One gold coin is in his grasp. His eyes meet it, and we see thoughtful deliberation. It is possible he is daydreaming about the benefits he can reap from it. Although his fellow knights may find him dull, he is hard-working and calm.

Possible events: Money will certainly come to you, but on the contrary might have some deadlock.

Personal growth: This is the time to take care of physical and routine essentials. In all aspects of life, now is the time to be practical, compassionate, patient, honest and dependable. Helping others is the best approach to attain both personal and professional progress.

About a person: The Knight of Pentacles is no different from other tarot knights in that he is ambitious and successful. The Knight of Pentacles is patient and always deliberate before acting, knowing what they want and how to attain it. Despite this, they move a little more slowly than the average person. Even if they don't make much money, they are good at money management. Their word is trustworthy. They keep their word when they commit to anything. This person can still be in school or be at the beginning stages of their job. They are going to be prosperous anyway.

Money: Money will come your way as a result of your great labour and sensible investment. This card can also imply property in specific cases. You must avoid risks, be prudent with your money, and maintain a stable financial situation. Instead of relying on windfall earnings, attempt to acquire things gently and consistently.

Love: This card represents consistency and commitment in a partnership. This partnership will be based on practical considerations such as sexual delights and financial stability. In these situations, you must stay honest and patient with yourself and your partner.

Career: This is the time to advocate for self-sufficiency. To be successful, you must rely on your hard work and endurance. This card also suggests that a job can yield fruitful results.

Farming, manufacturing or construction are examples of possible occupations.

Queen of Pentacles

Element: Earth

Astrological signs: Virgo, Capricorn, Taurus

Upright: Good income, sensible, sympathetic

Reversed: Possessive, fishy, objective

Card description: The Queen of Pentacles shows a beautiful woman seated on a throne and holding a golden coin. Flowers and trees are blooming all around her, creating a serene environment. Her throne is adorned by wild animals from all over the world, symbolising her close connection to nature and plenty. As a symbol of her boundless vitality and procreative potential, a rabbit leaps into the frame. As a result, the Queen of Pentacles represents a certain level of achievement and wealth. However, the rabbit serves as a warning that we should watch our step as we pursue this goal.

Possible events: The downward slope of bank balance, express ownership.

Personal growth: The Queen represents the physical world's dominance. The card urges you to gain control over your finances and possessions. Enjoy, care for, and accept your own body. Start meditating on the Queen if you want to make your dream a reality.

About a person: The Queen of Pentacles, as a person, is an outgoing, sensual, and loving person. She is trustworthy and sincere. Having achieved material success, she enjoys giving to others and sharing what she has. She also enjoys the outdoors and animals. The Queen of Pentacles' garden is a rich, organic haven of abundance that she has nurtured through her consistent, persevering, and diligent work. The Queen of Pentacles wants you to take stock of everything you've accomplished and all your accomplishments, no matter how small they may appear right now. You'll be able to see their significance when put into context and with no expectations other than to stay in the present.

Money: You can make financial gains through successful investments or business initiatives. If you want success, use your money and other resources constructively and creatively, focusing on collaborative financial endeavours. Try to handle your money wisely.

Love: The Queen of Pentacles depicts a mature relationship between people who are truthful in their feelings. Respect, fulfilment, sensual pleasure, protection, and mutual support will be the foundations of any association.

Career: The Queen represents collaborative ventures, coordination, and alliance, indicating that you have a competitive advantage in business and a good understanding of people management. Supplement financial incentives with a job. In a health-related industry, your work will benefit others, and people would rely on you for financial support.

King of Pentacles

Element: Earth

Astrological signs: Virgo, Capricorn, Taurus

Upright: Solitary, loyal, pragmatic

Reversed: Conservative, numb, envious

Card description: A man who is the King of Pentacles has lofty aspirations, finds fulfilment in worldly pursuits, and has achieved great success in life. The throne upon which reclines the king is carved with grapevines and bulls, and the robe he wears is embroidered with numerous depictions of grapevines. He has a refined, aristocratic air about him. This king has achieved material success, as evidenced by the many plants, vines, and flowers surrounding him. A sceptre rests in his right hand, while the coin bearing the pentacles is in his left. As if to emphasise his resolve and hard work, the castle can be seen in the background.

Possible events: Fate will overturn the situation of crisis to abundance, and kick off some bumper prize but enemies are watching you. Be careful.

Personal growth: There is a requirement for both organisation and practicality. Build up your resources and work towards becoming more self-sufficient. Ponder this for a while.

About a person: The King of Pentacles, as a person, is sophisticated, and uses a variety of skills to make the most of every circumstance. Everything the King of Pentacles touches turns to gold, creating enormous material fortune, almost like Midas. The King of Pentacles is so capable and dependable that others rely on him. He gives lavishly because he is confident that he will receive whatever he gives away, maybe more. In any circumstance, he offers stability while following his objectives all the way to completion. The King of Pentacles desires to spread the benefits of his achievement to others since he is proud of his accomplishments.

Money: You have the ability to achieve monetary security and success; however, you are the only one who can be responsible for your spending and savings habits. There is a good chance that you will find success and fortune in your life. This card indicates that you are in charge of the flow of money or are exercising financial mastery, possibly on a large scale. Now is the time to be well organised and to practise responsible financial management.

Love: This card represents a committed, long-term relationship between two people committed to each other's development and happiness. It is possible, though, that money, social standing and safety are the primary motivating factors in this relationship. A relationship can be secure and pleasant, but that does not mean it is exciting or romantic.

Career: The monarch is a symbol of success in the business world, whether by achieving a stable career path or effective management of material resources. You will be more likely to accomplish what you set out to accomplish if you are well organised, brave, honest and determined. Invest your time and effort into creating something that will last for a long time.

❑

CHAPTER 4

Keywords to Remember

The following charts would help you as a ready reckoner that you may refer to whenever you feel directionless or are not able to interpret anything. These keywords serve as a great tool to touch base with cards time and again. You may also stick a printout of these in your Tarot Manual (where you mention your own findings) and may refer to them time and again.

MAJOR ARCANA

CARD	KEYWORDS/MANTRA	PLANET/ ASTROLOGICAL ASSOCIATION	ELEMENT	CHAKRA
0 - THE FOOL	FRESH START, LEAP OF FAITH *'IT'S TIME TO EMBARK ON A BRAND-NEW BEGINNING.'*	URANUS	AIR	CROWN
1 - THE MAGICIAN	POWER, SKILL *'I HAVE ALL THE RESOURCES I NEED, INNER AND OUTER.'*	MERCURY	AIR	THROAT
2 - THE HIGH PRIESTESS	INTUITION, HIGHER WISDOM *'MY INNER KNOWING IS MY BEST GUIDE OF ALL.'*	MOON	WATER	THIRD EYE
3 - THE EMPRESS	FERTILITY, ABUNDANCE, CREATIVITY *'CONNECTING TO THE EARTH REMINDS ME THAT ABUNDANCE IS UNLIMITED.'*	VENUS	EARTH	HEART AND SACRAL
4 - THE EMPEROR	AUTHORITY, FATHER FIGURE *'I AM MY OWN AUTHORITY. I HAVE THE WILL AND THE POWER TO CREATE MY OWN LIFE'S STRUCTURE.'*	MARS/ARIES	FIRE	ROOT
5 - THE HIEROPHANT	RELIGION, GROUP IDENTITY *'I CHOOSE WHICH TRADITIONS I EMBRACE, AND HOW I DO IT.'*	VENUS/TAURUS	EARTH	THROAT
6 - THE LOVERS	LOVE, UNION, BONDS *'MY PERSONAL VALUES SYSTEM LEAD ME TO LOVE.'*	MERCURY/GEMINI	AIR	HEART

7 - THE CHARIOT	VICTORY, ASSERTION, MOMENTUM *'NO OBSTACLES WILL STOP ME NOW.'*	MOON/CANCER	WATER	THROAT
8 - STRENGTH	COURAGE, SELF-CONTROL *'STRENGTH BEGINS WITH THE CHOICE TO BE KIND TO ME.'*	SUN/LEO	FIRE	SOLAR PLEXUS
9 - THE HERMIT	SOUL-SEARCHING, SOLITUDE *'I HONOUR MY SPIRITUAL SELF.'*	CHIRON/VIRGO	EARTH	THIRD EYE
10 - THE WHEEL OF FORTUNE	KARMA, TURNING A CYCLE *'I RIDE THE WAVES OF LIFE.'*	JUPITER	FIRE	SOLAR PLEXUS
11 - JUSTICE	FAIRNESS, CAUSE AND EFFECT *'I GET WHAT I GIVE.'*	VENUS/ LIBRA	AIR	HEART
12 - THE HANGED MAN	LETTING GO, SUSPENSION *'IT'S TIME FOR A SACRED PAUSE. STILLNESS GRANTS PERSPECTIVE.'*	NEPTUNE	WATER	THIRD EYE
13 - DEATH	ENDINGS, BEGINNINGS *'I'M WILLING TO LET GO AND TO CHANGE.'*	PLUTO/SCORPIO	WATER	HEART
14 - TEMPERANCE	BALANCE, HEALING *'MY EXTREMES GUIDE ME TO FIND PEACE.'*	JUPITER/ SAGITTARIUS	FIRE	SOLAR PLEXUS
15 - THE DEVIL	BONDAGE, RESTRICTION *'I AM NOT A PUPPET.'*	SATURN/ CAPRICORN	EARTH	ROOT
16 - THE TOWER	SUDDEN CHANGE *'I SURRENDER TO THE STORM.'*	MARS	FIRE	CROWN
17 - THE STAR	HOPE, SPIRITUAL GUIDANCE *'THE UNIVERSE SHOWS ME THAT I CAN HAVE FAITH IN MY DREAMS.'*	URANUS/ AQUARIUS	AIR	CROWN

18 - THE MOON	ILLUSION, MYSTERY, DREAMS *'THE PATH MAY NOT BE CLEAR, BUT MY INTUITION LIGHTS THE WAY, ONE STEP AT A TIME.'*	NEPTUNE/PISCES	WATER	THIRD EYE
19 - THE SUN	SUCCESS, VITALITY, YOUTH *'I SHINE MY LIGHT ON THE WORLD AROUND ME AND MY RADIANCE ATTRACTS MORE SUCCESS.'*	THE SUN	FIRE	SOLAR PLEXUS
19 - JUDGEMENT	INNER CALLING *'THE DAILY CHOICES I MAKE NOW ALIGN ME WITH MY LIFE'S PURPOSE.'*	PLUTO	FIRE	CROWN
20 - THE WORLD	COMPLETION, ACCOMPLISHMENT *'WHAT I'VE BEEN WORKING FOR IS ALREADY DONE.'*	SATURN	EARTH	ROOT

MINOR ARCANA

CARD	OVERALL THEME	WANDS	CUPS	SWORDS	PENTACLES
ACE	POTENTIAL	INSPIRATION	INTIMACY	CLARITY	PROSPERITY
TWO	DUALITY	CHOICE	LOVE	DECISION	DECISION
THREE	UNITY	FORESIGHT	FRIENDSHIP	PAIN	TEAMWORK
FOUR	STABILITY	COMMUNITY	APATHY	REST	BUDGETING
FIVE	CHALLENGES	CONFLICT	LOSS	DEFEAT	POVERTY
SIX	GROWTH	RECOGNITION	YOUTH	TRANSITION	CHARITY/ GIVING
SEVEN	FAITH	STANDING YOUR GROUND	DREAMS/ FANTASIES	MAKING A BREAK FOR IT	MAKING INVESTMENTS

EIGHT	CHANGE	CHANGE/ TRAVEL/ NEWS	MOVING ON	ISOLATION	PATIENCE
NINE	FRUITION	RESILIENCE	FULFILMENT	ANXIETY	INDEPENDENT WEALTH
TEN	COMPLETION	BURDEN	MARRIAGE	ENDINGS/ DEFEAT	CULMINATION

COURT CARDS

CARD	THEME	WANDS	CUPS	SWORDS	PENTACLES
PAGE	MESSAGES	ENTHUSIASM	SYNCHRONICITY	CURIOSITY	NEW JOB
KNIGHT	MOTION	PASSION	ROMANCE	HASTE	ROUTINE
QUEEN	CREATIVITY	VIBRANCY	NURTURING	ASTUTE	ABUNDANCE/ CREATIVITY
KING	VISION	VISION	EMOTIONAL SELF-CONTROL	TRUTH	SECURITY

CHAPTER 5

Tarot Reading & Spreads

It is possible to use tarot cards for many purposes, including gaining insight into a problem or situation, gaining insight into the future, helping with meditation, or performing magical work.

A reading consists of drawing individual cards from a deck or laying out the cards in various patterns or arrangements, referred to as spreads. A reading can be as straightforward as choosing a card at random from the deck to serve as a source of inspiration during the day. Complex readings that involve multiple different spreads, can be done to examine a concern from a variety of angles, provide insight into more than one related issue, or give an overview of your life. These readings can be done for several different reasons.

Readings are clear and accurate based on the questions asked. Also, the questions need to be practical and relevant—else, a reader may not be able to relate to the readings with a clear mindset. For example, if a girl asks the tarot what kind of a man she will marry when she's thirteen, the tarot will respond based on the circumstances now, but the answer is unlikely to be very helpful. The actions and attitudes you take, in addition to external factors beyond your control, will have an impact on the events that take place between now and then, thereby influencing the course of your future.

Do not approach a tarot reading with scepticism or amusement; also, do not test the oracle to see if it will correctly respond to a question whose answer you already know. A tarot reading is not a game you can play in your living room. Consider a reading to be a private performance before an all-knowing stage audience. Honour both the sage who provided the information and the place from which it originated. Be honest in your reading, and have faith that the tarot will give you sound guidance, no matter what kind of reading you do.

The more pertinent the issue is to you and the more specific your inquiry is, the higher the probability that you will be given sound guidance.

Here are some tips.

- ✦ Do not ask several questions at once.
- ✦ Begin by inquiring about what is most prominent in your mind, and then, if you so desire, move on to other subjects. The tarot will frequently respond to the issue weighing the heaviest on your mind, even if your question is on another matter.
- ✦ If you are unsatisfied with the response, you should not ask the same question again, hoping to elicit a response that better suits your needs.
- ✦ If you do not understand the answer, ask for more clarification or a different question that is related to the topic at hand.

- ✦ Never attempt to read something when you are overly tired or preoccupied with something else.
- ✦ Consuming alcohol or other substances that alter mood can affect a reading and produce a confusing or inaccurate response.

Laying out the cards

The reading will start with either the reader or the querent choosing a significator, which is a card that represents the individual for whom the reading is being done. Some people purposefully choose a card that reflects some aspect of their identity, such as their astrological sign, age, profession, or other factors. For instance, a banker who is forty-six years old may be able to identify with the King of Pentacles. Others favour randomly selecting a card from the deck as the significator instead of doing the draw.

Even though the significator is typically a card depicting a 'person' (such as a court card, The High Priestess, or The Emperor), this is not always the case. In most cases, a card selected at random will accurately portray your current state of being or the primary focus of your attention at the time of the reading. If you are ready to embark on an adventure, your gut reaction may be to choose a knight as your significator. On the other hand, if you are anxious about a legal matter, you might go with Justice. This card reveals something about you and connects you with the reading in a very personal way. At the same time, it reveals something about the reading.

Take a few minutes to calm down and get your bearings before you arrange the cards. While you are shuffling the cards, you should think about the question or concern you have. If you want to, you can blow on them. When you are ready, cut the cards using your 'other' hand, which is the hand you do not typically write with. Next, lay out your spread starting from the top of the second pile with the cards facing the same direction. You can choose to deal the cards face down in front of you after shuffling them first if that is more convenient for you. Pick out some cards from the fan and lay them out in a spread. You can use as few as one card or as many as all of them.

The methods or spreads described below are a few of my most beloved spreads. I recommend that you try them all and then stick with the ones that work best for the goals you have set. You are free to make any alterations you see fit, or you can design your very own unique spreads too.

Single-Card Method

This reading is the simplest of all readings, and it can be done every morning to provide you with food for thought throughout the day or to provide guidance about a particular matter, particularly an ongoing one such as a relationship or job.

Continue with the steps from above, then cut the deck and flip the card on top of it. That concludes today's lesson or piece of advice from you. You might find it helpful to meditate with this card or to keep it displayed in a location where you will see it frequently throughout the day.

Past-Present-Future Spread

Cut the deck after shuffling it, then draw cards from the top of the second pile. Place three face-up cards in a row from the left to the right. The card on the left denotes the history of the situation or its origins, the card in the middle explains the situation now, and the card on the right reveals what will happen soon.

Four-Card Spread

Cut the deck after shuffling the cards. Place four face-up cards in a row, moving from left to right. The card on the left indicates the current situation, the second card illustrates the difficulty or obstacle lying in wait for you, the third card recommends the course of action you should take, and the card on the right reveals the result/outcome.

This or That Spread

When you are trying to decide between two possibilities, use this straightforward strategy. The cards are cut and shuffled. One card to demonstrate what you are likely to experience if you choose to go with the option. The second card may suggest the outcome if you do not go like that option. Feel free to lay two more cards in the same format for a clearer reading in case you cannot interpret the first set clearly.

Yes-No Spread

You can answer questions of a yes-or-no nature by using this method. Cut the deck after shuffling the cards. Begin by flipping over each card in turn and placing it in a pile. Continue doing this until you reach an ace or have counted thirteen cards. Put a stop to it and start a new pile; arranging the cards in the same fashion as before. When you turn over an ace or when you have laid out thirteen cards, you should stop. Create a third pile using the same method as before.

The answer is unquestionably 'yes' if the result is—three aces turned over in your hand. Two aces suggest ambiguity; this may indicate that the situation is still developing or could go either way. If there is only one ace or none, it is impossible to determine the answer currently.

The suits of the aces will frequently describe the nature of your concern in one way or another. The card on top of a stack of thirteen will reveal the circumstances surrounding the question or offer some possible solutions.

Once, I did a reading for a woman in the recovery phase after having surgery for cancer. She wanted to know if the cancer had disappeared. The response from the tarot was two ace cards and a pile of thirteen cards with the Queen of Pentacles on top. The way the question was answered led me to believe that the answer was yes, but that she also needed to take good care of her body to prevent cancer from coming back.

Karma-Dharma Spread

This spread sheds light on a specific aspect of your life by illuminating the opportunities available and revealing the obstacles preventing you from taking advantage of them. Cut the deck after shuffling the cards.

Place the first card on the table facing up. This card offers insight into the present circumstances or the question asked in the reading. You should expose a second card and place it on top of the first one. This card represents your dharma, which can be considered your life's goals, calling, potential or options. It tells you what you should aim for or work hard to accomplish. Put a card with the face upside facing down beneath the first card. This card reveals your karma, which consists of your self-limiting thoughts, deeds, and other experiences from the past (either from your childhood or from previous lifetimes) obstructing or undermining your progress.

Simple Cross

This design combines the Karma-Dharma Spread with the Past-Present-Future Spread to create the pattern. After shuffling and cutting the deck, the cards should be arranged as follows:

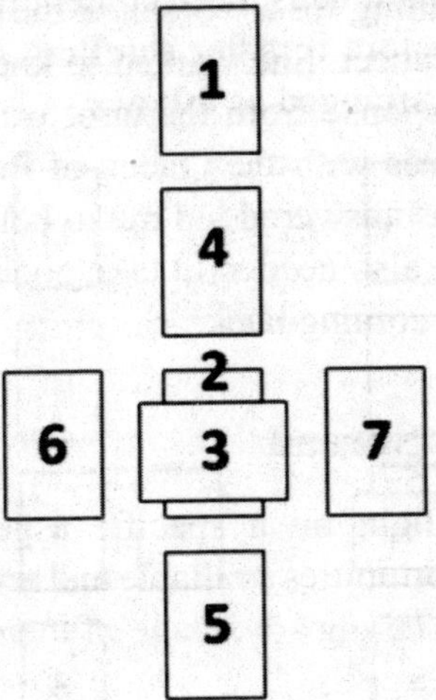

Card 1 is significator.

Card 2 represents the current circumstance or the topic of the reading.

Card 3 represents the challenge or possibility that is affecting the current circumstance.

Card 4 represents your hopes and dreams, opportunities, goals and potential, as well as what you want most and should be working hard to achieve.

Card 5 represents what is beneath you, including any weaknesses, old baggage, attitudes, or behaviours preventing you from moving forward.

Card 6 refers to the recent past.

Card 7 represents the near future.

Celtic Cross Spread

The Celtic Cross is the most common layout for reading tarot cards and can be used to gain insight into virtually any situation or problem. Note that it adds more content than the Simple Cross Spread that came before it. After shuffling and cutting the deck, the cards should be arranged as follows:

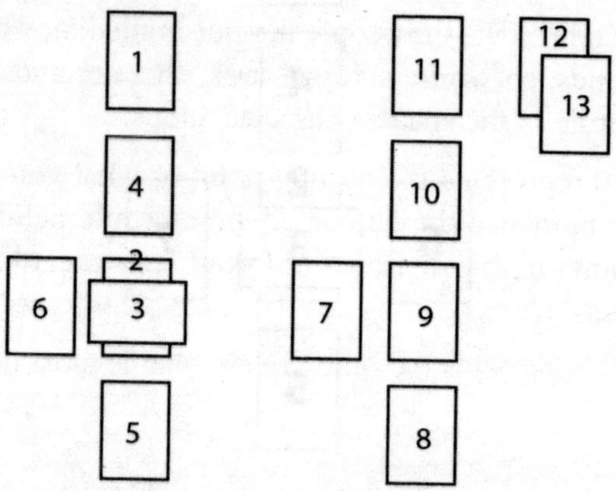

Card 1 is significator.

Card 2 represents the current circumstances or the topic of the reading.

Card 3 represents the challenge or chance that is currently influencing the situation.

Card 4 represents your hopes and dreams, opportunities, goals and potential, as well and also what you want most and should be working hard to achieve.

Card 5 represents challenges you have faced in the past, areas in which you struggle, what's beneath you, and things that may be preventing you from moving forward.

Card 6 represents the end of the present, the recent past, and what has just occurred or is about to leave your life.

Card 7 represents the beginning of the future, or what will happen in the not-too-distant future, typically within the next few days or so.

Card 8 represents the environment or the conditions you will encounter in the days, weeks, or months ahead regarding the topic of the reading you are doing.

Card 9 represents the people in your immediate environment, such as friends, co-workers, loved ones, enemies and others, who will play a role in the situation as it develops.

Card 10 represents the turning point or what you could do to produce or influence the outcome; some people believe that this position shows both your hopes and your fears regarding the topic of the reading.

Card 11 represents the outcome or what is most likely to take place.

Cards 12 and 13 represent a further amplification of the outcome (if necessary), which can explain the subject of the reading in greater detail or expand on it altogether; however, in most cases, these cards are only used when the outcome card is a card with great importance.

Horoscope Spread

If you want a glimpse of what the coming birthday year has in store for your client, you should consider using this spread on their birthday. In addition to this, it has the potential to offer guidance and information on constructively managing the various aspects of life. Different houses in an astrological chart or horoscope depict certain facets of a person's life. After shuffling and cutting the cards, place one card, with the face up, in each of the twelve houses, so that the circle is complete.

Determine the meaning of the cards based on the characteristics of the different houses in a horoscope. If 'The Sun' falls as Card #10, for example, it indicates that you are clear about your professional goals and that the public views you as a strong, confident and creative leader. If The Moon falls as

Card #4, it indicates that you may have mood swings related to different things or situations. The Three of Pentacles appearing in position number #6 may indicate that effectively putting your abilities to use will enable you to successfully complete a portion of the work you have been assigned. This spread shows specific outcomes or events in the areas of life that correspond to particular houses or give advice about how to make use of the relevant energies and abilities.

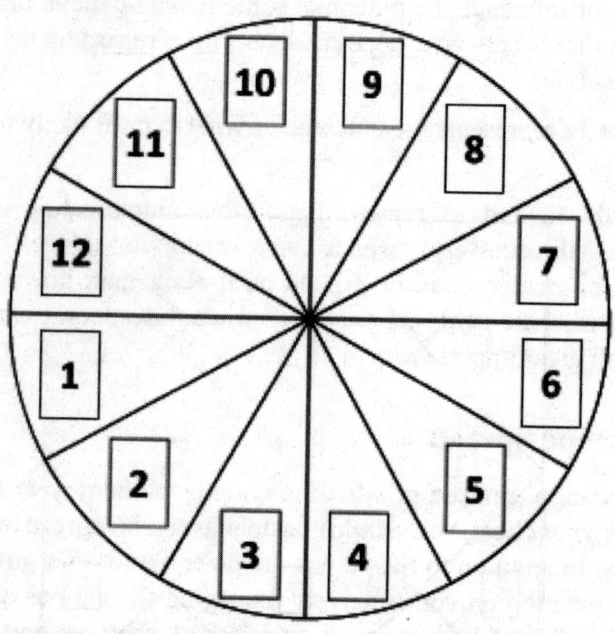

Some people in India also arrange these cards in a way it is read in the North Indian style horoscope so that you can memorise the meanings easily. The cards are arranged as shown in Fig B so that they correspond to the 12 houses of the horoscope as displayed in Fig A.

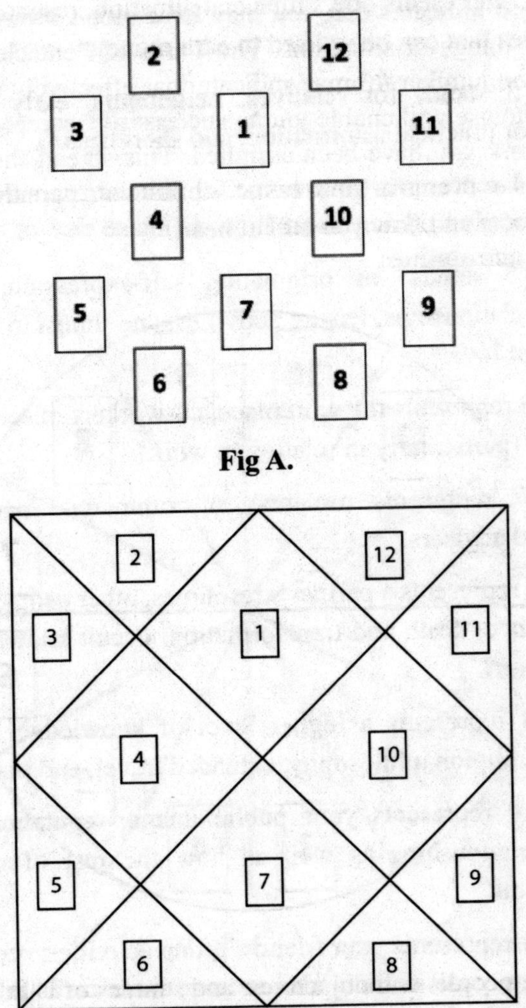

Fig A.

Fig B.

Card 1 is a symbol of your outward appearance, how you want to be perceived by others, and the first impression you make on other people.

Card 2 represents one's financial situation, resources, values, and abilities that can be utilised to earn money.

Card 3 stands for relatives, neighbours, early education, mundane or practical information, and short trips.

Card 4 represents your home, childhood, parents, sense of security, roots and how you feel at heart.

Card 5 stands for originality, self-expression, children, romantic relationships, leisure activities, and things to which you devote your love.

Card 6 represents the workplace, co-workers, responsibilities and health (particularly in relation to work).

Card 7 represents romantic or commercial partnerships, brokers and advisers.

Card 8 represents a partner's resources, other people's money, an inheritance, death and transformation, occult knowledge, and hidden power.

Card 9 represents a higher level of knowledge, advanced education, religion, philosophy, extended travel, and publishing.

Card 10 represents your public image, reputation, career, business relationships as well as how the rest of the world perceives you.

Card 11 represents your friends, group activities, professional organisations, goals and objectives, and sources of validation and encouragement.

Card 12 represents things that are hidden from view, such as resources, aspects of oneself that have not been fully developed, enemies hidden from view, one's shadow self, and things that work against one.

Feng Shui Spread

Feng shui practitioners use a map called a bagua, which has eight sides, to perform an analysis of your home. This pattern makes use of that map. According to the principles of Feng Shui, different parts of your home are associated with different aspects of your life. After shuffling and cutting the cards, place one card, displaying its front side, in each of the nine sectors, also known as gua.

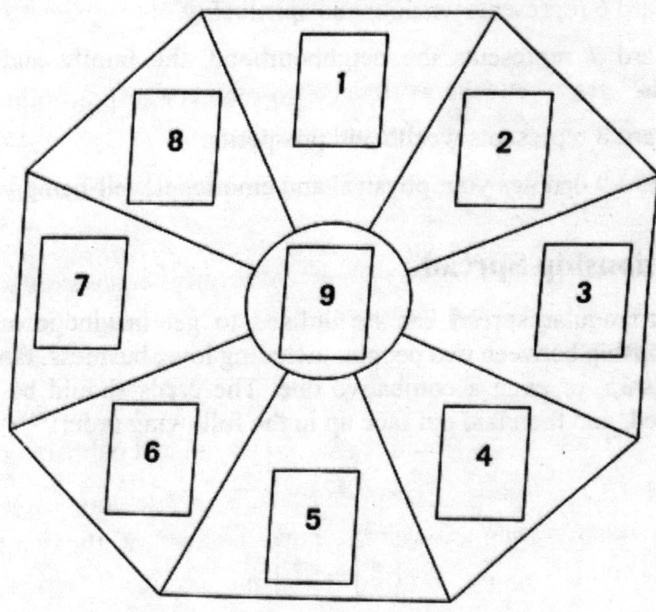

Consider the cards in light of the guas that each card represents. For instance, if The Star came up as Card #1, it indicates that you should maintain a positive outlook on your future because it is likely that you will achieve success and recognition. If you draw the Seven of Swords as your sixth card, it may be a sign that you have a distinctive spiritual or intellectual perspective and should walk on your own path.

Card 1 indicates fame, public image, and a bright future. Card2representsromanticrelationships,includingmarriageandlove. Card 3 represents creative endeavours, including the birth of children, and the act of expressing oneself.

Card 4 represents helpful individuals, including friends, co-workers, and travellers.

Card 5 represents the individual, their identity, professional endeavours, and the meaning of ones.

Card 6 represents wisdom and spirituality.

Card 7 represents the neighbourhood, the family and the friends.

Card 8 represents wealth and prosperity.

Card 9 denotes your physical and emotional well-being.

Relationship Spread

This triangular spread can be utilised to get insight into any relationship between two people, including love, business, family, friendship, or even a combative one. The cards should be cut, shuffled, and then laid out face up in the following order:

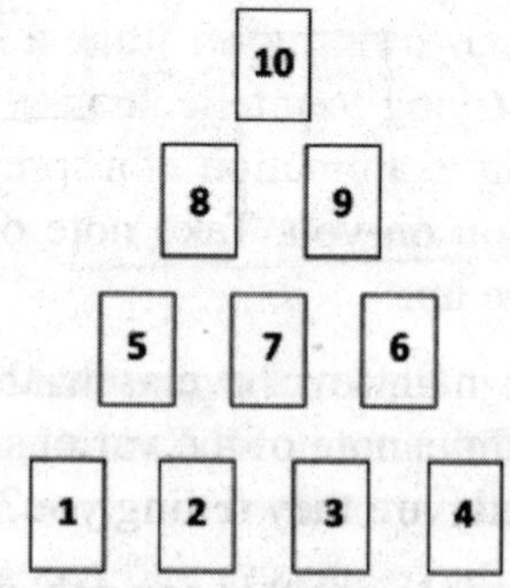

Card 1 represents the past, the basis upon which the relationship is built, and the karmic connection that exists between the parties involved in the relationship.

Card 2 refers to the existing problem or predicament.

Card 3 represents the challenge or the opportunity that this relationship presents.

Card 4 indicates how you should approach this challenge or opportunity.

Card 5 represents your part in the relationship and what you bring to it.

Card 6 represents the other person's role in the relationship as well as the contributions that they make to it.

Card 7 represents the entity that you created together.

Card 8 represents what you truly desire or anticipate from the partnership.

Card 9: What the other person actually wants from the relationship and what they expect from it.

Card 10 represents the final result.

Interpreting the cards

Using symbolic language, the tarot can have a direct conversation with your subconscious or intuition. Take a few moments to look at the cards without trying to intellectualise anything about them before beginning your examination of a spread. Allow the pattern to leave an impression on you. Take note of any sensations and realisations that come up.

Beginning with a high-level overview, then gradually moving into more specifics. Take note of the various hues and pictures on the cards. What exactly are they telling you?

Does one suit predominate? Is any suit absent? The suits offer a description of fundamental energies or modes of operation, in addition to the topic of the reading and the factors that are having an impact on the situation.

Do you have a lot of different court cards in your hand? This either indicates that there are many people around you or that other people play a crucial role in the situation.

Are there more than half as many Major Arcana cards as in the spread? The appearance of Major Arcana cards suggests that fate or other forces not under your control are at work and are directing the situation. The development of one's spirit or inner self might be more important than attaining physical results.

Think about the numbers printed on the cards. Do any numbers tend to be more common? These can provide insight into cycles or the degree to which a situation has progressed.

Investigate potential links between the cards. For example, do specific types of cards tend to show up in the 'past' positions of the deck? Is there an implication of development or advancement moving from the 'past' cards to the 'future' cards? A knight occupying a position from the past in a spread and a queen occupying a position from the future in the same spread, for instance, demonstrates progression over the time covered by the reading.

In the final step, analyse the significance of each individual card by taking into account not only its position in the spread but also its connections to the other cards and any other relevant factors.

Let your intuition guide you. Follow your instincts and go with what you think a card means, even if what you think is different than what the 'experts' say. Readings of the tarot are highly personal and should be regarded as a means of communicating with one's own inner knowing. In this sense, they are like dreams.

You should keep a record of everything you read in a journal. By doing so, you will be able to gain insight from them and improve your capacity for interpretation.

Reversed cards

Some of the cards may be upside down as you handle and shuffle them. They 'look reversed' when you lay them out. Many theories and explanations of reversed cards are presented in tarot publications.

In most cases, the reversal of a card indicates that there is either an obstruction, an imbalance, or an improper utilisation of the energy. For instance, the Six of Swords in an upright position can represent a progression, success in overcoming challenges, and advancement to more favourable stages. This card, when turned upside down, could mean avoiding difficult situations rather than confronting them head-on.

There is a school of thought among tarot researchers that suggests that flipped cards describe the 'shadow side' of the energies; what is hidden behind the expression on the surface, or issues one does not wish to acknowledge or address. Some people believe that the meaning of a card when it is turned upside down is the exact opposite of what it means when it is upright.

You should focus solely on the upright cards at first, at least until you have gained a better understanding of the tarot. If you draw a card with its face facing the opposite direction, simply flip it over and read it as usual. You will eventually be able to investigate the meanings of reversed cards and arrive at your own conclusions about them.

Note: *I personally keep all my cards arranged in the upright position so as not to be confused with reversed ones. Also, this approach purposely helps me reflect upon those cards that appear in a reversed position. Those energies help me look at the root cause of the problems.*

How often should you do readings?

Your motivation to learn something, the circumstances of your life at the time, the kind of information you look for, the kind of reading you do, and a host of other factors can all influence that. But the question here could be framed in this way—how often should you read for someone, and how often could you do it for yourself?

Those who wish to take up tarot professionally would need to read the cards several times a day. My suggestion is, once you have finished performing a reading for the first client—wrap your cards in a cloth after shuffling them several times so that they release the energies that they were holding for the client and pack them in the box where you keep them. For the next reading, always wash your hands or sprinkle some holy water in your hands. Then take the cards, shuffle them and start with the spread.

Coming to the question about how often can you read for yourself? A general reading can be done at least four times a year. Some people in the West do it on the equinoxes and the solstices, while I tell my students to do that at least once every quarter. A reading could also be done on your birthday. A glimpse into the upcoming year can be gained using the Horoscope Spread, which was covered earlier in this chapter.

Every month, to get a better overall picture, you could also do a Celtic Cross Spread for yourself. If you require guidance on a specific topic, you may use the Celtic Cross Spread or another one that seems more pertinent to the question at hand. When you are working on a problem, you may sometimes lay out more than one spread so that you get a clear answer or can approach it from different angles.

There are times when the cards become exhausted. It is possible that you overworked them or asked them the same question so many times that there is nothing else they can tell you about the situation at this time. When this occurs, you may find that the cards you choose have no apparent connection to the situation at hand. This could be very frustrating. When it is time to take a break, I frequently look at the Four of Swords or the Ten of Swords card in my deck. Put the cards away for a couple of days and give them some time to relax. You ought to probably give yourself some time off as well. If you do decide to continue conducting readings during this time, you should switch to a new deck of cards or meditate with your own cards for some time till you feel an equilibrium inside you.

❑